Stop Funding
Uncle Sam's
Retirement

GET A PLAN THAT'S SIMPLE
AND EASY TO UNDERSTAND

ROBERT MAGGI & CHRIS MAGGI

This document discusses general concepts for retirement planning, and is not intended to provide tax or legal advice. Individuals are urged to consult with their tax and legal professionals regarding these issues. This handbook should ensure that clients understand a) that annuities and some of their features have costs associated with them; b) that income received from annuities is taxable; and c) that annuities used to fund IRAs do not afford any additional measure of tax deferral for the IRA owner.

Printed in the United States of America

First Printing, 2014

Gradient Positioning Systems, LLC
4105 Lexington Avenue North, Suite 110
Arden Hills, MN 55126 (877) 901-0894

Gradient Positioning Systems, LLC, Robert and Chris Maggi are not affiliated with or endorsed by the Social Security Administration or any government agency.

TABLE OF CONTENTS

ACKNOWLEDGMENTS

We would like to thank all our clients who have been so trusting and loyal over the years. This book is dedicated to you. We are also deeply thankful for our wives, Anna and Dawn. They have given us the support, love, confidence and encouragement that has allowed us to make positive differences in the lives of our clients in the retirement planning business.

Thanks also to Darren Maggi who consistently provides support and insight into the creative design of our marketing and advertising material. His dedication & passion creating flyers, postcards and business cards has enabled us to display our business to make it simple and easy to understand.

Our acknowledgements would not be complete without recognizing the talented team of staff members at Maggi Tax Advisory & Financial Group. Special thanks to Dottie, our office manager. When we asked God to send us an office manager, he sent us the most caring, respectful, organized and polite lady who now oversees and supervises our three locations. Our tax preparers, Jeanne, Lisa and Bob who make our tax seasons possible each and every year – thank you. Thanks to Josie, who assists us with office procedures, and thanks to all our clients who we have assisted in developing a plan for their retirement. We appreciate your trust and confidence in us.

Above all, we want to thank God for making everything possible. We would like to thank all the wonderful supportive and creative team of Nick Stovall, Mike Binger, Nate Lucius and Gradient Positioning Systems, LLC for their contributions to this project.

ABOUT MAGGI TAX ADVISORY AND FINANCIAL GROUP

The financial advisory business that father and son team Robert and Chris Maggi have spent over a decade building is unlike any other. Maggi Tax Advisory and Financial Group works for their clients, not for their clients' money. Far too many of their competitors cannot say the same and it is their business model and philosophy that keeps their ultimate focus solely on the distinct needs and goals of every client. When it comes to financial planning, there is no exact manual outlining the "12 steps to success". Instead, there is simply education and a guiding hand, both of which are readily offered by Robert and Chris in the form of the Maggi Plan. It's a simple retirement plan you can understand.

The Maggi Plan is the result of Robert and Chris's nearly 40 years of combined financial expertise and provides clients with custom-tailored investment strategies to help them accomplish their personal and financial goals. What makes the Maggi Plan truly unique is its adherence to the principle that the client will be the best architect of his or her financial future. The role of the advisor should be to simply assist in supporting and maintaining that plan. Ultimately, the Maggi Plan allows for the client to create comprehensive, easy to understand, and effective financial strategies, which are uniquely suited to meeting the particular requirements of their situation.

In many ways, this innovative financial advisory approach represents the perfect balance of Robert and Chris's distinctive, yet complementary, skill sets and personalities. Robert has had a nearly lifelong career within the financial world so when Chris was in college and decided he wanted to follow suit and work on Wall Street, it came as no surprise. Quickly, however, Chris realized that many people put their money in the market not because it was the decision best suited to meet their financial needs, but because that was all they knew to do with their assets. It became all too apparent that people need help to develop a greater understanding of financial strategies so they can better protect themselves, their families, and their futures and Maggi Tax Advisory and Financial Group provides just that.

Robert and Chris have crafted a financial advisory approach that is comprehensive and attentive, not transactional. Most financial professionals operate within either the investment, tax, or insurance sector, which means the strategies and products they offer to clients are limited to their field. At Maggi Tax Advisory and Financial Group, all three of these divisions exist under one roof: clients have the largest possible range of options to draw from as they design their plans, ensuring they end up with the one that is right for them, their families, and their money. Robert and Chris are true proponents for the importance of being a *complete* financial advisor and the Maggi Plan is wholly reflective of that belief.

Ultimately, Robert and Chris's financial philosophy is a simple one: they endeavor to make financial planning as simple as possible by removing the confusion from it and encouraging people to ask questions. As fear is removed and understanding is added, the right plan becomes visible. Robert and Chris champion this idea not only to their clients, but to the greater public as well. Robert and Chris produce, write and host a weekly radio show, "The Maggi Tax and Financial Hour" every Saturday and Tuesday.For more than seven years, this father and son radio show has encouraged listeners to raise their hands and ask the questions that matter to them. Robert and Chris have devoted their professional lives to furthering the financial education and support of their clients.

INTRODUCTION

It's a simple and readily apparent fact that we all lead busy lives: the world moves quickly and so must we. Most of us have spent our days being propelled from one task to another: we went to school to get a job, we found a job to get a house; the list of things we do to get to the places we want to go is endless. Some of us probably embarked on these endeavors with both a clear destination and route in mind, while others may have begun with a destination but figured out their way as they went along. Neither of these methods should be considered the "right" or "wrong" way because life is about enjoying the journey not maintaining an itinerary. Time and again, the moments we cherish the most are the ones we least expected. As we've all learned, it's hard to find joy in the present when we're already looking ahead towards what's next.

While this perspective can absolutely help you lead a full and happy life, strict adherence to it may result in a full and happy life, but only up to the moment right before you retire. Retirement is one part of life's journey that can really only be enjoyed when it has a set destination and a carefully charted course to get you there.

If you enter into your retirement with no plan, even if you have ample financial assets, you are setting yourself up for unnecessary failure and stress. Not only will you have no way of knowing if you will have enough money to comfortably support your retirement but, more importantly, you will not have a recourse of action to take if your money dwindles faster than you age. In other words, it's difficult to enjoy the ride when you don't know how long it's going to last. By taking the time to look ahead and make a plan for your retirement now, you give yourself the gift of being able to actually enjoy it later.

You've invested an immense portion of your time and energy into your career and the way you approach your retirement will determine the extent to which you can finally reap your returns. **This is *your* money that you've worked incredibly hard for, now is the time to put it into a *plan of your own design* to make it work for you.** Many people are fearful they don't have enough money only because they're worried they won't know how to make it last for the rest of their lifetime: you don't need to be one of them. By sitting down with a financial professional and analyzing your current financial position, you can begin to turn the lights on in your retirement by developing a comprehensive and easy to understand plan with a purpose that can take you where you want to go.

A NEW WORLD

Although you have spent your entire life working and earning money, retirement represents an incomparably unique financial challenge. Prior to your retirement, your fiscal life is dictated by an earning and saving paradigm that you've most likely been following since you received your first allowance. However, once you retire you will no longer be earning a paycheck that you can save but you will still need money. At this point, you will have to transition into relying on an income and asset leveraging paradigm to use the funds you previously earned and saved to generate an income and preserve your assets for you.

In of itself, simply having to make that mental and financial shift would be a tall order. As it is, however, there is much more work to be done. Not only do you have to entirely re-conceptualize and reorganize your finances to ensure that you will be able to continue to provide for you and your family, but you also have to do so within a volatile and shifting economic landscape that is riddled with taxes, inflation, fluctuating interest rates, and other financial uncertainties. This is not a time to make a mistake: the line between a good retirement decision and a bad one can sometimes be razor-thin and its ramifications can be profound and lasting. Although this poses a distinctive challenge, with a little planning, guidance, and education, it is one you are more than capable of surmounting.

When it comes to retirement, there is no universally successful plan because each plan should be carefully customized to address the unique goals and needs of its retiree. Every person's situation is different so every plan should be adjusted to satisfy those requirements. However, the plans most successful at providing a secure and long-lasting retirement will utilize a holistic perspective to maintain a healthy balance between safe money and long-term growth to generate a variety of guaranteed income sources with the least amount of tax implications possible. What's more is that each vehicle and strategy will have been carefully and deliberately selected because it is the tool most capable of satisfying a specific need or helping to accomplish a specific goal.

The first step towards creating *your* retirement plan is to understand where you and your assets are positioned. In other words, you should work with a financial professional to take an "x-ray" of your portfolio and other holdings so you can dissect exactly where you're at and what you need. Even before you decide where it is that you want your money to take you, and certainly before you begin designing how you want it to take you there, you need to know where your money currently is, how much risk it's exposed to, and what it's doing there.

Essentially, you don't know what you don't know, so until you understand what benefits and failings exist in your current finances you can't begin to craft a plan that will be able to utilize or compensate for them. Once you understand your assets, you need to decide what you hope to accomplish with your retirement plan and begin to build your plan accordingly. Is the purpose of your plan geared more towards accumulation so your children might inherit a larger legacy? Or is it more focused on leveraging financial products to create several reliable sources of retirement income?

Basically, the strategies and tools employed by your plan will be drawn from the trifecta of retirement planning: taxes, investment, and insurance. As there is possibly no greater threat to the success of your retirement plan than the ever-increasing blight of taxes across our economy, your plan should strive to provide you with as much tax-free or tax-advantaged income as possible. In order to help your money accumulate and keep pace with inflation, your plan could use a well-managed and diversify portfolio. To design your plan with reliable income sources that are minimally taxed, a variety of insurance products could be used.

WHERE DO WE GO FROM HERE?

The information outlined in this book will help inform you about some of the financial strategies and vehicles that are at your disposable. By staying well-informed and working with a financial professional, you can create a comprehensive, purposeful, and easy-to-understand retirement plan that is specifically crafted to meet your needs. You and your family's futures are worth securing. Why settle for anything less than the perfect fit?

1

ORGANIZING YOUR ASSETS

"Will we have enough money for retirement?"

How do you know if your Social Security benefit, savings, and other assets will be enough to support you throughout your retirement? If you're anything like Wallace and Mackenzie, you hope it will be. The couple just entered their sixties and they're beginning to imagine what their life might look like 10 years down the road. Ideally, they would both like to retire before then, but they're not sure when it would make the most sense to do so. They know they will have their Social Security benefits to rely on, but not only are they unsure about how much that will be worth, they don't know when or how to file so they can get the most out of their benefit. Wallace has a pension that he will be able to begin drawing from when he's 68 years old, but he doesn't like his job very much and would really like to retire before then. Mackenzie, on the other hand, has a 401(k) but she doesn't know much about it other than the fact that a small amount of her paycheck is automatically deposited into it every month. How will all these different assets come together to create a comfortable and secure retirement?

Wallace and Mackenzie's predicament is a fairly common one. It may even remind you of yours. While you may have built up a 401(k), an IRA, and Social Security benefits, do you know what your financial picture really looks like?

Consider retirement as the part of a process that began the first day we began our careers. With this view, there are four main phases of retirement planning: contribution, accumulation, distribution, and transfer. The first two, contribution and accumulation, are the phases we spend the vast majority of our lives in and, depending on the type of retirement account you have, it's possible for both phases to occur simultaneously. Most of us spend our lives working and contributing money to our retirement, waiting for the day when our working income ceases and we reach the point of relying on our assets for income, which marks our entrance into the distribution phase of our financial plan. The moment this phase begins can be referred to as the retirement **cliff**.

As the name implies, transitioning into the distribution phase of your plan represents a significant change because saving money for retirement, which is what you have spent your life doing, and *planning* your retirement are two different things. When you enter the distribution phase, you will no longer be earning a working income but you will still need an income. At this point, you will need to have a solid financial strategy in place that will accommodate your day-to-day need for funds by leveraging your existing assets to generate an income. Structuring your assets to create an income-generating retirement requires a different approach than earning income via the workforce.

You spend your entire working life hoping what you put into your retirement accounts will help you live comfortably once you clock out of the workforce for good. The key word in that sentiment and the word that can make retirement feel like a looming problem instead of a rewarding life stage, is **hope**. You hope you'll have enough money. Add to this the complexities of taxes, required minimum distributions (RMDs) from IRAs and legacy planning, and you can begin to see why successfully jumping off the retirement cliff requires more than hope. They need a focused and well-executed plan.

Leaving your retirement up to chance is unadvisable by nearly any standard, yet millions of people find themselves *hoping* instead of planning for a happy ending. With information, tools and professional guidance, creating a successful retirement plan can put you in control of your financial management.

Now that you know there's more to saving and planning for retirement than filing for your Social Security benefit and drawing income from your 401(k), you can begin to **create a strategy for your retirement** that can have a significant impact on your financial landscape after you stop drawing a paycheck. Understanding how to manage your assets entails risk management, risk diversification, tax planning and income planning preparation throughout your life stages. These strategies can help you leverage more from each one of the hard-earned dollars you set aside for your retirement.

Some people file for Social Security on day one of their retirement. Others rely on supplemental income from an IRA or another retirement account. Working with a financial professional can help you determine your best course of action.

AN OLD IDEA IN A NEW WORLD

While there are some basic investment concepts that have stood the test of time, most strategies that work adapt to changing conditions in the market, in the economy and the world, as well as changes in your personal circumstances. The reality is that investment strategies and savings plans that worked in the past have encountered challenging new circumstances that have turned them on their heads.

In the early 1990s, interest rates were high and market volatility was low. Essentially, this meant you could either invest in the market to take advantage of its growth potential but still avoid exposing your investment to a lot of risk, or you could invest in a financial product to play it safe but interest rates were high enough so that your money would still be able to comfortably accumulate. At that time, because you could expose yourself to an acceptable amount of risk or an acceptable fixed rate, you had a wide variety of investment options with which you were likely to be fairly successful. Basically, it was difficult to make a mistake during that time period. Today, you don't have those options. Market volatility is at an all-time high while interest rates are at all-time lows. They are so far apart from each other that it is hard to know what to do with your money. This means yesterday's investment rules may not work today. Not only could they hamper achieving your goals, they may actually harm your financial situation.

For example, the Great Recession of 2008 highlighted how old investment ideas were not only ineffective but incredibly destructive to the retirement plans of millions of Americans. The dawn of an entirely restructured health care system brings with it new options and challenges that will undoubtedly change the way insurance companies provide investment products and services.

Perhaps the most important lessons investors learned from the Great Recession is that not understanding where your money is invested (and the potential risks of those investments) can work against you, your plans for retirement and your legacy. Saving and investing money isn't enough to truly get the most out of it. You must have a simple approach to managing your assets.

Essentially, managing your money and your investments is an ongoing process that requires customization and adjusting to a changing world. And make no mistake; the world is always changing. What worked for your parents or even your parents' parents was probably good advice back then. People in retirement or approaching retirement today need new ideas and professional guidance because current interest rates are at historic lows and the volatility of the market is higher than ever. There is no overlapping acceptable rate between the two, making both options less than ideal. *Because of this uncertain financial landscape, wise investment strategies are more important now than ever.*

This unique situation requires fresh ideas and investment tools that haven't been relied on in the past. Investing the way your parents did will not pay off. The majority of investment ideas used by financial professionals in the 1990s aren't applicable to today's markets. That kind of investing will likely get you in trouble and compromise your retirement. Today, you need a better PLAN.

I HOPE SO MONEY VS. I KNOW SO MONEY

Now that you have a better idea of the overall financial picture, let's look at the money that gives it color. There are essentially two kinds of money: *I Hope So Money* and *I Know So Money*. Everyone can divide their money into these two categories. Some have more of one kind than the other. The goal isn't to eliminate one kind of money but to balance them as you approach retirement.

I Hope So Money is, as the name indicates, money that you *hope* will be there when you need it. In other words, it is money that is at risk because it fluctuates with the market and doesn't come with a minimum guarantee. It is subject to investor activity, stock prices, market trends, buying trends, etc. This money is exposed to more risk but also has the potential for more reward. Because the market is subject to change, you can't really be sure what the value of your investments will be worth in the future. In other words, you can't really *rely* on it at all. This doesn't mean you shouldn't have some money invested in the market, but it would be dangerous to assume you can know what it will be worth in the future. For this reason, it is referred to as I Hope So Money because it represents what you would like to get out of your investments.

I Hope So Money is an important element of a retirement plan, especially in the early stages of planning when you can trade volatility for potential returns, and when a longer investment timeframe is available to you. In the long run, time can smooth out the ups and downs of money exposed to the market. Working with a professional and leveraging a long-term investment strategy has the potential to create rewarding returns from I Hope So Money. Some common examples of I Hope So Money include:

- Stock market funds, including index funds
- Mutual funds
- Variable annuities
- REITS

I Know So Money is money that you know you can count on. It is made up of dependable, low-risk or no-risk money to create investments that you can count on. This money isn't exposed to

The VIX, or volatility index, of the market represents expected market volatility. When the VIX drops, economic experts expect less volatility. When the VIX rises, more volatility is expected.

the level of volatility as the asset types noted above so you can more confidently count on having this money when you need it.

For example, Social Security is one of the most common forms of I Know So Money because income you draw or will draw from it is guaranteed. You have paid into Social Security your entire career, and you can rely on that money during your retirement. Unlike the market, rates of growth for I Know So Money are dependent on 10-year treasury rates. The 10-year treasury, or TNX, is commonly considered to represent a very secure and safe place for your money, hence I Know So Money. The 10-year treasury drives key rates for things such as mortgage rates or CD rates. I Know So Money may not be as exciting as I Hope So Money, but it is safer. Examples of I Know So Money are:

- Government backed bonds
- Savings and checking accounts
- Fixed income annuities
- CDs
- Treasuries
- Money market accounts

Knowing the difference between I Hope So Money and I Know So Money is an important step towards a successful retirement plan. Ideally, the rates of return on I Hope So Money and I Know So Money would have an overlapping area that provided an acceptable rate of risk for both types of money. However, as you know from earlier remarks, market volatility is high whereas interest rates

---

1. *VIX is a trademarked ticker symbol for the Chicago Board Options Exchange (CBOE) Market Volatility Index, a popular measure of the implied volatility of S&P 500 index options. Often referred to as the fear index or the fear gauge, it represents one measure of the market's expectation of stock market volatility over the next 30 day period. (wikipedia.com)*

2. *The CBOE 10-Year Treasury Note (TNX) is based on 10 times the yield-to-maturity on the most recently auctioned 10-year Treasury note.*

are low. Consequently, you can't just invest all your money in one place or the other because you would run the risk of losing all your money if the market dropped or your money would lose value because the interest rate is barely keeping pace with inflation. In other words, you need to balance the amount of risk to which you are exposed by having both I Know So Money and I Hope So Money.

Before you can know *how* to balance your risk, however, you first need to know how much risk you're exposed to, period. Many investors don't know how vulnerable to risk their assets may or may not be. It is helpful to organize your assets so you can have a clear understanding of how much of your money is at risk and how much is in safer holdings.

> » *Diane has a small brokerage account that she adds to whenever she's able. When she changed jobs a couple years ago, at age 58, Diane transferred her 401(k) assets into an IRA. Just a few years from retirement, she is now beginning to realize that nearly every dollar she has saved for retirement is subject to market risk.*
>
> *Intuitively, she knows that the time has come to shift some assets to an alternative that is safer, but how much is the right amount?*

The average investor needs to accumulate assets to create a retirement plan that will first accommodate their day-to-day income needs income during retirement and also allows for legacy planning. Managing your risk by having a balance of I Hope So Money vs. I Know So Money is a good start that will put you ahead of the curve. But how much I Know So Money is enough to secure your income needs during retirement, and how much I Hope So Money is enough to allow you to continue to benefit from an improving market? How much money do you need to maintain your lifestyle? When do you need it?

In short, how do you begin to know how much risk you should be exposed to?

RULE OF 100

Determining the amount of risk that is right for you is dependent on a number of variables. Your age, health, comfort level, and financial need among others will all play a role in setting your assets' level of risk exposure. You need to feel comfortable with where and how you are investing your money, and your financial professional is obligated to help you make decisions that put your money in places that fit your risk criteria. While there is no single approach to determine investment risk there are some helpful guidelines.

The Rule of 100 is a general rule that helps shape asset diversification* for the average investor. The rule states that the number 100 minus an investor's age equals the percentage of assets they should have exposed to risk.

The Rule of 100: 100 - (your age) = the percentage of your assets that should be exposed to risk (Hope So Money)

For example, if you are a 30-year-old investor, the Rule of 100 would indicate that you should be focusing on investing primarily in the market and taking on a substantial amount of risk in your portfolio. The Rule of 100 suggests that 70 percent of your investments should be exposed to risk.

100 - (30 years of age) = 70 percent

Asset Diversification disclosure – Diversification and asset allocation does not assure of guarantee better performance and cannot eliminate the risk of investment loss. Before investing, you should carefully read the applicable volatility disclosure for each of the underlying funds, which can be found in the current prospectus.

As you can see from the formula, risk tolerance generally reduces as you get older. Much of the flexibility that comes with investing earlier in life is related to *compounding*. Compounded earnings can be incredibly powerful over time. The longer your money has time to compound, the greater your wealth will be. This is what most people talk about when they refer to putting their money to work. This is also why the Rule of 100 favors risk for the young. If you start investing when you are young, you can invest smaller amounts of money in a more aggressive fashion because you have the potential to make a profit in a rising market and you can harness the power of compounding earnings. When you are 40, 50 or 60 years old, that potential becomes less and less and you are forced to have more money at lower amounts of risk to realize the same returns. **It basically becomes more expensive to prudently invest the older you get.**

You risk not having a recovery period the older you get, so should have less of your assets at risk in volatile investments. You should shift with the Rule of 100 to protect your assets and ensure that they will provide you with the income you need in retirement. Consider the following examples to further see the relationship between age and the rule of 100.

Perhaps when you were age 30 and starting your career as in the example above, it made sense to have 70 percent of your money in the market: you had time on your side. You had plenty of time to save more money, work more and recover from a downturn in the

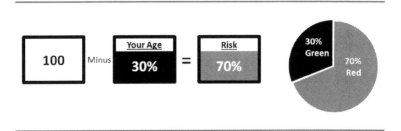

market. Retirement was ages away, and your earning power was increasing. And indeed, younger investors should take on more risk for exactly those reasons. The potential reward of long-term involvement in the market outweighs the risk of investing when you are young.

Additionally, if a 40 year old were to lose 30 percent of their retirement portfolio in a market downturn this year, they would have 20 or 30 years to recover it. On the other hand, someone who is 68 years old would only have five to 10 years (or less) to make the same recovery. That new circumstance changes your whole retirement perspective. At age 68, it's likely that you simply aren't as interested in suffering through a tough stock market. There is less time to recover from downturns, and the stakes are higher. The money you have saved is money you will soon need to provide you with income, or is money that you already need to meet your income demands.

Finally, let's look at another example that illustrates how managing your risk exposure becomes more critical as you age. An 80-year-old investor who is retired and is relying on retirement assets for income, for example, needs to depend on a solid amount of I Know So Money. The Rule of 100 says an 80-year-old investor should have a maximum of 20 percent of his or her assets at risk. Depending on the investor's financial position, even less risk exposure may be required. You are the only person who can make this kind of determination, but the Rule of 100 can help. Everyone has their own level of comfort. Your Rule of 100 results will be based on your values and attitudes as well as your comfort with risk.

Of course, your ability to bear risk is dependent on more than your age. Now, not every 30-year-old should have exactly 70 percent of their assets in mutual funds and stocks. The Rule of 100 is based on your chronological age, not your "financial age," which could vary based on your investment experience, your aversion or acceptance of risk and other factors. While this rule isn't an ironclad solution to anyone's finances, it's a pretty good place to start.

Once you've taken the time to look at your assets with a professional to determine your risk exposure, you can use the Rule of 100 to make changes that put you in a more stable investment position — one that reflects your comfort level.

What's more is that the Rule of 100 can apply to overarching financial management and to specific investment products that you own as well. Take the 401(k) for example. Many people have them, but not many people understand how their money is allocated within their 401(k). An employer may have someone who comes in once a year and explains the models and options that employees can choose from, but that's as much guidance as most 401(k) holders get. Many 401(k) options include target date funds that change their risk exposure over time, essentially following a form of the Rule of 100. Selecting one of these options can often be a good move for employees because they shift your risk as you age, securing more I Know So Money when you need it.

A financial professional can look at your assets with you and discuss alternatives to optimize your balance between I Know So Money and Hope So Money.

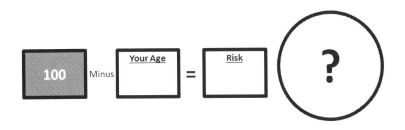

CHAPTER 1 RECAP //

- There is money you hope you'll have in the future, and there's money you know you'll have in the future. Make sure you know how much you need when you retire.
- Make sure you know how much risk each of your assets is exposed to so you can then understand how to balance each asset for risk.
- Your exposure to risk is ultimately determined by you.
- Use the Rule of 100 as a general guiding principle when determining how much risk your retirement investments should be exposed to (100 - [your age] = [percentage of your investments that can comfortably exposed to risk])

2

THE COLOR OF MONEY

"Can we afford to retire now?"

The fact of the matter is that a lot of people don't know their level of exposure to risk. As we have seen, it's more important than ever to know which of your assets are at risk. High market volatility and low treasury rates make for challenging financial topography. Navigating this financial landscape starts with simple asset management that takes into account your specific needs and options.

Visually organizing your assets is an important and powerful way to get a clear picture of what kind of money you have, where it is and how you can best use it in the future. This process is as simple as listing your assets and assigning them a color according to which kind of money it is and its level of risk. For our purposes, I Know So Money (which is safer and more dependable) is green. I Hope So Money (which is exposed to risk and fluctuates with

Green Money	Red Money
"Green Money" is safer.	"Red Money" is at risk.
This is money that offers a minimum guarantee but it may pose risks other than market risk.	This is money that can go up or down in value. It may pose risk if it is not properly managed to serve a specific purpose in a comprehensive plan.

the market) is red. A financial professional can help you better understand the color of the money in your investment portfolio. Work with your financial professional to create a comprehensive inventory of your assets to understand what you are working with before making any decisions. This may be the first time you have ever sat down and sorted out all of your assets, allowing you to see how much money you have at risk in the market. Comparing the color of your investments will give you an idea of how near or far you are from adhering to the Rule of 100.

Over the course of your lifetime, it is likely that you have acquired a variety of assets. Assets can range from money that you have in a savings account or a 401(k), to a pension or an IRA. You have earned money and have made financial decisions based on the best information you had at the time. When viewed as a whole, however, you might not have an overall strategy for the management of your assets.

Even if you feel that you have plenty of money in your 401(k) or IRA, not knowing how much *risk* those investments are exposed to can cause you major financial suffering. Take the market crash of 2008 for example. In 2008, the average investor lost 30 percent of their 401(k). If more people had shifted their investments away from risk as they neared retirement age (i.e. the Rule of 100), they may have lost a lot less money going into retirement.

When using the Rule of 100 to calculate your level of risk, your financial age might be different than your chronological age, however. The way you organize your assets depends on your goals and your level of comfort with risk. Whatever you determine the appropriate amount of risk for you to be, you will need to organize your portfolio to reflect your goals. If you have more Red Money than Green Money, in particular, you will need to make decisions about how to move it. You can work with a financial professional to find appropriate Green Money options for your situation. As you organize your assets and take a closer look at them, you might realize your Green Money has more than one shade.

SHADES OF GREEN:
I NEED NOW MONEY AND I NEED LATER MONEY
Money that you need to depend on for income is Green Money. Once you have satisfied your need for immediate income at the beginning of your retirement, however, you may have money left over. If you do, you will see that there are two types of Green Money: money used for income and money used for accumulation to meet your income needs in five, 10 or 20 years.

Money needed for income is **I Need Now Money**. It is money you need to meet your basic needs, to pay your bills, your mortgage if you have one, and the costs associated with maintaining your lifestyle. Money used for accumulation is **I Need Later Money**. It's money that you don't need now for income, but will need to rely on down the road. It's still Green Money because you will rely on it later for income and will need to count on it being there. I Need Later Money represents income your assets will need to generate for future use.

When planning your retirement, it is vital to decide how much of your assets to structure for income and how much to set aside to accumulate to create I Need Later Money. You must figure out if your income and accumulation needs are met. Your I Need Now and I Need Later Money are top priorities. I Need Now Money, in particular, will dictate what your options for future needs are.

Basically, Green Money becomes much more important as you age. While you want to reduce the amount of Red Money you have and to transition it to Green Money, you don't necessarily need all of it to generate income for you right away. But investing heavily in Red Money and gambling all of your assets on the market is incredibly risky no matter where you fall within the Rule of 100. Money in the market can't be depended on to generate income, and a plan that leans too heavily on Red Money can easily fail, especially when investment decisions are influenced by emotional reactions to market downturns and recoveries. Not only is this an unwise plan, it can be incredibly stressful to an investor who is gambling everything on stocks and mutual funds.

But a plan that uses too much Green Money avoids all volatility and can also fail. Why? Investing all of your money in Certificates of Deposit (CDs), savings accounts, money markets and other low return accounts may provide interest and income, but that likely won't be enough to keep pace with inflation. If you focus exclusively on income from Green Money and avoid owning any stocks or mutual funds in your portfolio, you won't be able to leverage the potential for long-term growth your portfolio needs to stay healthy and productive. This is where the Rule of 100 can help you determine how much of your money should be invested in the market to anticipate your future needs.

Ultimately, you need to balance your Red Money and Green Money so that you can be assured that, on a guaranteed basis, your retirement plan will satisfy your daily income need. You need to structure your money so it can provide you with income and accumulate, but not at the expense of your risk tolerance. This will come from determining the right amount and ratio of Green and Red Money for you at your stage of retirement planning. The only way to be confident that your plan will accomplish this is to know the numbers: you need to create a budget that accounts for your monthly expenses and income.

CREATING AN INCOME PLAN

Evaluating your income needs will help you find the most efficient and beneficial way to address them, which will have impacts on your lifestyle, your asset accumulation and your legacy planning after you retire. When you have identified your income need, you will know how much to structure for income and how much to be set aside for accumulation. This is where your Green Money comes into play: the safer, more reliable assets that you have accumulated that can be designed to provide you with a steady income.

Always remember that on day one of your retirement, you will need a steady and reliable supply of income from your Green Money. Satisfying that need for daily income entails first knowing *how much you need* and *when you will need it.*

How Much Money Do You Need? While this amount will be different for everyone, the general rule of thumb is that a retiree will require 70 to 80 percent of their pre-retirement income to maintain their lifestyle. Once you know what that number is, the key becomes matching your income need with the correct investment strategies, options and tools to satisfy that need.

When Do You Need Your Money? If you need income to last 10 years, use a tool that creates just that. If you need a lifetime of income, seek a tool that will do that and won't run out.

So how do you figure out how much you need and when you need it? When you take health care costs, potential emergencies, plans for moving or traveling, and other retirement expenses into account, you can really give your calculator a workout. You want to maximize retirement benefits to meet your lifetime income needs. An Investment Advisor can help you answer those questions by working with you to customize an income plan. When you optimize your income planning, you will see that it's not about *finding* more money; it's about leveraging what you already have to generate the income you need.

As we determined earlier in Chapter 1, the most important thing you need to do as you create an income plan is to take care to avoid too much exposure to risk. You can start by meeting with an Investment Advisor to organize your assets. Get your Green Money and Red Money in order and balanced to meet your needs. If the market goes down 18 percent this afternoon, you don't want that to come out of what you're relying on for next year's income.

OPTIMIZING RISK AND FINDING THE RIGHT BALANCE

Determining the amount of risk that is right for you depends on your specific situation and it starts by using the Rule of 100 to dissect your particular financial position to discover what the right amount of risk is for you.

Remember that the Rule of 100 is just a baseline. Use it as a starting point for figuring out where your money should be. If you're a 50-year-old investor, the Rule of 100 suggests that you have 50 percent Green Money and 50 percent Red Money. Most 50-year-olds are more risk tolerant, however. There are many reasons why someone might be more risk tolerant, not the least of which is feeling young! Experienced investors, people who feel they need to gamble for a higher return, or people who have met their retirement income goals and are looking for additional ways to accumulate wealth are all candidates for investment strategies that incorporate higher levels of risk. In the end, it comes down to your personal tolerance for risk. How much are you willing to lose?

Consulting with a financial professional is often the wisest approach to calculating your risk level. A professional can help determine your risk tolerance by getting to know you, asking you a set of questions and even giving you a survey to determine your comfort level with different types of risk. Here's a typical scenario a financial professional might pose to you:

"You have $100,000 saved that you would like to invest in the market. There is an investment product that could turn your $100,000 into $120,000. That same option, however, has the potential of losing you up to $30,000, leaving you with $70,000."

Is that a scenario that you are willing to enter into? Or are you more comfortable with this one:

"You could turn your $100,000 into $110,000, but have the potential of losing $15,000, leaving you with $85,000."

Your answer to these and other types of questions will help a financial professional determine what level of risk is right for you. They can offer you investment strategies and management plans that reflect your financial age.

Take a moment to think about your income goals:

What is your lifestyle today? Would you like to maintain it into retirement? Are you meeting your needs? Are you happy with your lifestyle? What do you really *need* to live on when you retire? How are you going to structure your income flow during retirement?

Ultimately, crafting the retirement plan that is right for you is a numbers game: your risk tolerance is an important indicator of what kinds of investments you should consider, but if the returns from those investments don't meet your retirement goals, your income needs will likely not be met. For example, if the level of risk you are comfortable with manages your investments at a 4 percent return and you need to realize an 8 percent return, your income needs aren't going to be met when you need to rely on your investments for retirement income. The truth of the matter is that some people will have the luxury of maintaining or improving their lifestyle, while others may have to make decisions about what they need versus what they want during their retirement. If the numbers say that you need to be more aggressive with your investing, or that you need to modify your lifestyle, it becomes a choice you need to make.

Organizing your assets, understanding the color of your money, and creating an income and accumulation plan for retirement can quickly become an overwhelming task. The fact of the matter is that financial professionals build their careers around understanding the different variables affecting retirement financing. A professional may encourage you to be more aggressive with your investment strategy by taking on more risk in order to give you the potential of earning a greater return. If taking more risk isn't an option that you are comfortable with, then the discussion will turn to how you can earn more money or spend less in order to align your needs with your resources more closely.

Enlisting the help of a Registered Investment Advisor means working with a professional who is legally obligated to help you make financial decisions that are in your best interest and fall within your comfort zone. Taking steps toward creating a retirement plan is nothing to take lightly. By leveraging tax strategies, properly organizing your assets, and accumulating helpful financial products that help you meet your income and accumulation needs, you are more likely to meet your goals. You might have a million dollars socked away in a savings account, but your neighbor, who has $300,000 in a diverse investment portfolio that is tailored to their needs, may end up enjoying a better retirement lifestyle. Why? They had more than a good work ethic and a penchant for saving. They had a simple approach to retirement asset allocation.

CHAPTER 2 RECAP //

- There are two types of money: Green and Red. Green Money represents assets that are "safer" and more reliable. Red Money represents assets that are exposed to risk.
- There are two types of Green Money: *I Need Now and I Need Later.* It is important to structure your investments to provide you with income now and later.
- Working with a Registered Investment Advisor will help you compose a clear and concise inventory of your assets, and learn how much they are worth, what rules apply to them, and how they are structured for risk.
- A Registered Investment Advisor can help you structure your investments so as to reflect your risk tolerance.
- Working with an Investment Advisor means working with a professional who is legally obligated to help you make financial decisions that are in your best interest and fall within your comfort zone.
- The foundation of a retirement strategy depends on knowing how much money you need and when you need it.

3

UNDERSTANDING SOCIAL SECURITY

One kind of Green Money that most Americans can rely on for income when they retire is Social Security. If you're like most Americans, Social Security is or will be an important part of your retirement income and one that you should know how to properly manage. As a first step in creating your income plan, a financial professional will take a look at your Social Security benefit options. Social Security is the foundation of income planning for anyone who is about to retire and is a reliable source of Green Money in your overall income plan.

> » *Gale had worked full-time nearly her entire adult life and was looking forward to enjoying retirement with her husband, kids and grandkids. When she turned 62, she decided to take*

> *advantage of her Social Security benefits as soon as they became available.*
>
> *A couple of years later, she was organizing some of the paperwork in her home office. She came across an old Social Security statement, and remembered the feeling of filing and beginning a new phase in her life.*
>
> *However, as she looked over the statement, she realized in retrospect that she might have been better off waiting to file for benefits. She had saved enough to wait for benefits, and if she had, her monthly benefit could have been quite a bit more.*
>
> *When she was in the process of retiring, there were so many other decisions to make. It seemed very straightforward to file right away. She made a note to call the Social Security Administration to see if it was possible to change her monthly benefit to the larger amount.*

Unfortunately, Gale's story is not unusual. When you begin planning your retirement and are looking for income streams to tap into, your Social Security benefit will often be used to form that foundation. However, just like any vehicle, Social Security has its own set of operating procedures that must be considered if you want to get the most possible mileage out of it. Had Gale waited to file for Social Security, her monthly benefit could have been higher, which would have meant less money had to be pulled from her nest egg to use as I Need Now income. Instead, that money could have been put to work for other uses.

One of the most important things to take away from Gale's story is that, practically speaking, Gale cannot change her Social Security benefit. Once you file for Social Security and begin collecting your monthly benefit, you are permanently locked into that amount. This underscores the importance of taking the time to thoroughly consider all of your options and make sure that filing for your benefit at that time is the strategy best-suited to fulfilling that purpose. While there is one exception to this rule it can often be difficult to take advantage of it: if you have taken less than 12 months of payment and repay all the benefit checks you receive, you can defer filing and reapply later, when your benefits could be potentially higher. It's also crucial to understand that your Social Security benefit is subject to taxes and to take this into account as you consider when and how to file.

As you can see, there is more to filing for your Social Security benefit than just filling out the correct paperwork. However, many people don't understand this. As the facts below exemplify, many people rely on Social Security, but they don't know how to do so in the most effective manner:

- 90 percent of Americans age 65 and older receive Social Security benefits.*
- Social Security provides 39 percent of income for retired Americans.*
- Claiming Social Security benefits at the wrong time can reduce your monthly benefit by up to 57 percent.**
- 43 percent of men and 48 percent of women claim Social Security benefits at age 62.**
- 74 percent of retirees receive reduced Social Security benefits.**
- In 2013, the average monthly Social Security benefit was $1,261. *The maximum benefit for 2013 was $2,533. The $1,272 monthly benefit reduction between the average and the maximum is applied for life.****

---

*http://www.ssa.gov/pressoffice/basicfact.htm
**When to Claim Social Security Benefits, David Blanchett, CFA, CFP® January, 2013
***http://www.socialsecurity.gov/pressoffice/factsheets/colafacts2013.com

There are many aspects of Social Security that are well known and others that aren't. When it comes time for you to cash in on your Social Security benefit, you will have many options and choices. Social Security is a massive government program that manages retirement benefits for millions of people. Experts spend their entire careers understanding and analyzing it. Luckily, you don't have to understand all of the intricacies of Social Security to maximize its advantages. You simply need to know the best way to manage your Social Security benefit. You need to know exactly what to do to get the most from your Social Security benefit and when to do it. Taking the time to create a roadmap for your Social Security strategy will help ensure that you are able to exact your maximum benefit and efficiently coordinate it with the rest of your retirement plan.

There are many aspects of Social Security that you have no control over. You don't control how much you put into it, and you don't control what it's invested in or how the government manages it. However, you do control when and how you file for benefits. The real question about Social Security that you need to answer is, "When should I start taking Social Security?" While this is the all-important question, there are a couple of key pieces of information you need to track down first.

Before we get into a few calculations and strategies that can make all the difference, let's start by covering the basic information about Social Security which should give you an idea of where you stand. Just as the foundation of a house creates the stable platform for the rest of the framework to rest upon, your Social Security benefit is an important part of your overall retirement plan. The purpose of the information that follows is not to give an exhaustive explanation of how Social Security works, but to give you some tools and questions to start understanding how Social Security affects your retirement and how you can prepare for it. Let's start with eligibility.

Eligibility. Understanding how and when you are eligible for Social Security benefits will help clarify what to expect when the time comes to claim them.

To receive retirement benefits from Social Security, you must earn eligibility. In almost all cases, Americans born after 1929 must earn 40 quarters of credit to be eligible to draw their Social Security retirement benefit. In 2013, a Social Security credit represents $1,160 earned in a calendar quarter. The number changes as it is indexed each year, but not drastically. In 2012, a credit represented $1,130. Four quarters of credit is the maximum number that can be earned each year. In 2013, an American would have had to earn at least $4,640 to accumulate four credits. In order to qualify for retirement benefits, you must have earned a minimum number of credits. Additionally, if you are at least 62 years old and have been married to a recipient of Social Security benefits for at least 12 months, you can choose to receive Spousal Benefits. Although 40 is the minimum number of credits required to begin drawing benefits, it is important to know that once you claim your Social Security benefit, there is no going back. Although there may be cost of living adjustments made, you are locked into that base benefit amount forever.

Primary Insurance Amount. You can think of your Primary Insurance Amount (PIA) like a ripening fruit. It represents the amount of your Social Security benefit at your Full Retirement Age (FRA). Your benefit becomes fully ripe at your FRA, and will neither reduce nor increase due to early or delayed retirement options. If you opt to take benefits before your FRA, however, your monthly benefit will be less than your PIA. You will essentially be picking an unripened fruit. On the one hand, waiting until after your FRA to access your benefits will increase your benefit beyond your PIA. On the other hand, you don't want the fruit to over-ripen, because every month you wait is one less check you get from the government.

Full Retirement Age. Your FRA is an important figure for anyone who is planning to rely on Social Security benefits in their retirement. Depending on when you were born, there is a specific age at which you will attain FRA. Your FRA is dictated by your year of birth and is the age at which you can begin your full monthly benefit. Your FRA is important because it is half of the equation used to calculate your Social Security benefit. The other half of the equation is based on when you start taking benefits.

When Social Security was initially set up, the FRA was age 65, and it still is for people born before 1938. But as time has passed, the age for receiving full retirement benefits has increased. If you were born between 1938 and 1960, your full retirement age is somewhere on a sliding scale between 65 and 67. Anyone born in 1960 or later will now have to wait until age 67 for full benefits. Increasing the FRA has helped the government reduce the cost of the Social Security program, which pays out more than a half trillion dollars to beneficiaries every year!*

While you can begin collecting benefits as early as age 62, the amount you receive as a monthly benefit will be less than it would be if you wait until you reached your FRA or surpass your FRA. It is important to note that if you file for Social Security benefit before your FRA, ***the reduction to your monthly benefit will remain in place for the rest of your life.*** You can also delay receiving benefits up to age 70, in which case your benefits will be higher than your PIA for the rest of your life.

At FRA, 100 percent of PIA is available as a monthly benefit.

At age 62, your Social Security retirement benefits are available. For each month you take benefits prior to your FRA, however, the monthly amount of your benefit is reduced. ***This reduction stays in place for the rest of your life.***

---

http://www.ssa.gov/pressoffice/basicfact.htm

At age 70, your monthly benefit reaches its maximum. After you turn age 70, your monthly benefit will no longer increase.

Year of Birth	Full Retirement Age
1943-1954	66
1955	66 and 2 months
1956	66 and 4 months
1957	66 and 6 months
1958	66 and 8 months
1959	66 and 10 months
1960 or later	age 67*

ROLLING UP YOUR SOCIAL SECURITY

Your Social Security income "rolls up" the longer you wait to claim it. Your monthly benefit will continue to increase until you turn 70 years old. But because Social Security is the foundation of most people's retirement, many Americans feel that they don't have control over how or when they receive their benefits. As a matter of fact, only 4 percent of Americans wait until after their FRA to file for benefits! This trend persists, despite the fact that every dollar you increase your Social Security income by means less money you will have to spend from your nest egg to meet your retirement income needs! For many people, creating their Social Security strategy is the most important decision they can make to positively impact their retirement. ***The difference between the best and worst Social Security decision can be tens of thousands of dollars over a lifetime of benefits — up to $170,000!***

Deciding NOW or LATER: Following the above logic, it makes sense to wait as long as you can to begin receiving your Social Security benefit. However, the answer isn't always that simple. Not

---

http://www.ssa.gov/OACT/progdata/nra.html

everyone has the option of waiting. Many people need to rely on Social Security on day one of their retirement. In fact, **nearly 50 percent of 62-year-old Americans file for Social Security benefits.** Why is this number so high? Some might need the income. Others might be in poor health and don't feel they will live long enough to make FRA worthwhile for themselves or their families. It is also possible, however, that the majority of folks taking an early benefit at age 62 are simply under-informed about Social Security. Below are some general guidelines to consider when you're trying to decide when to file:

File Immediately if You:
- Find your job is unbearable.
- Are willing to sacrifice retirement income.
- Are not healthy and need a reliable source of income.

Consider Delaying Your Benefit if You:
- Want to maximize your retirement income.
- Want to increase retirement benefits for your spouse.
- Are still working and like it. (This is especially important because if you take your Social Security benefit before your FRA but continue working in a job that earns more than $15,000 per year, for every $2 you earn over $15,000, the government will withhold $1. Once you reach your FRA, you can make as much money as you want).
- Are healthy and willing/able to wait to file.

So if you decide to wait, how long should you wait? Lots of people can put it off for a few years, but not everyone can wait until they are 70 years old. Your individual circumstances may be able to help you determine when you should begin taking Social Security. If you do the math, you will quickly see that between ages 62 and 70, there are 96 months in which you can file for your Social

Security benefit. If you take into account those 96 months and the 96 months your spouse could also file for Social Security, the number of different strategies for structuring your benefit, you can easily end up with more than 20,000 different scenarios. It's safe to say this isn't the kind of math that most people can easily handle. Each month would result in a different benefit amount. The longer you wait, the higher your monthly benefit amount becomes. Each month you wait, however, is one less month that you receive a Social Security check.

The goal is to maximize your lifetime benefits. That may not always mean waiting until you can get the largest monthly payment. Taking the bigger picture into account, you want to find out how to get the most money out of Social Security over the number of years that you draw from it. Don't underestimate the power of optimizing your benefit: the difference between the BEST and WORST Social Security election can easily be between $30,000 to $50,000 in lifetime benefits. ***The difference can be very substantial!***

If you know that every month you wait, your Social Security benefit goes up a little bit, and you also know that every month you wait, you receive one less benefit check, how do you determine where the sweet spot is that maximizes your benefits over your lifetime? Financial professionals have access to software that will calculate the best year and month for you to file for benefits based on your default life expectancy. You can further customize that information by estimating your life expectancy based on your health, habits and family history. If you can then create an income plan (we'll get into this later in the chapter) that helps you wait until the target date for you to file for Social Security, you can optimize your retirement income strategy to get the most out of your Social Security benefit. How can you calculate your life expectancy? Well, you don't know exactly how long you'll live, but you have a better idea than the government does. They rely on averages to make their calculations. ***You have much more personal*** *information about your health, lifestyle and family history than they do.* You can use that knowledge to game the system and beat all the other people who are making uninformed decisions by filing early for Social Security.

While you can and should educate yourself about how Social Security works, the reality is you don't need to know a lot of general information about Social Security in order to make choices about your retirement. What you do need to know is exactly *what to do to maximize your benefit.* Because knowing what you need to do has huge impacts on your retirement! For most Americans, Social Security is the foundation of income planning for retirement. Social Security benefits represent nearly 40 percent of the income of retirees.* For many people, it can represent the largest portion of their retirement income. Not treating your Social Security benefit as an asset and investment tool can lead to sub-optimization of your largest source of retirement income.

Let's take a look at an example that shows the impact of working with a financial professional to optimize Social Security benefits:

> » *Jeff and Holly Stein are a typical American couple who have worked their whole lives and saved when they could. Jeff is 60 years old, and Holly is 56 years old. They sat down with a financial professional who logged onto the Social Security website to look up their PIAs. Jeff's PIA is $1,900 and Holly's is $900.*
>
> *If the Steins cash in at age 62 and begin taking retirement benefits from Social Security, they will receive an estimated $492,000 in lifetime benefits. That may seem like a lot, but if you divide that amount over 20 years, it averages out to be just shy of $25,000 per year. The Steins are accustomed to a more significant annual income than that. To make up the*

---

*http://www.ssa.gov/pressoffice/basicfact.htm

difference, they will have to rely on alternative retirement income options. They will basically have to depend on a bigger nest egg to provide them with the income they need.

If they both wait until their FRA, they will increase their lifetime benefits to an estimated $523,700. This option allows them to achieve their Primary Insurance Amount, which will provide them a $33,000 annual income.

After learning the Steins' needs and using software to calculate the most optimal time to begin drawing benefits, the Steins' financial professional determined that the best option for them drastically increases their potential lifetime benefits to $660,000!

*By using strategies that their financial professional recommended, they increased their potential lifetime benefits by as much as **$148,000.** There's no telling how much you could miss out on from your Social Security if you don't take time to create a strategy that calculates your maximum benefit. For Jeff and Holly, the value of maximizing their benefits was the difference between night and day. While this may seem like a special case, it isn't uncommon to find benefit increases of this magnitude. You'll never know unless you take a look at your own options.*

Despite the importance of knowing when and how to take your Social Security benefit, many of today's retirees and pre-retirees may know little about the mechanics of Social Security and how they can maximize their benefit.

So, to whom should you turn for advice when making this complex decision? Before you pick up the phone and call Uncle Sam, you should know that the Social Security Administration (SSA) representatives are actually prohibited from giving you election advice! In fact, SSA representatives in general are trained to focus on monthly benefit amounts, not the lifetime income for a family.

MAXIMIZING YOUR LIFETIME BENEFIT

As discussed earlier, calculating how to maximize **lifetime benefits** is more important than waiting until age 70 for your maximum **monthly benefit amount.** It's about getting the most income during your lifetime. Professional benefit maximization software can target the year and month that it is most beneficial for you to file based on your life expectancy.

The three most common ages that people associate with retirement benefits are 62 (Earliest Eligible Age), 66 (Full Retirement Age), and 70 (age at which monthly maximum benefit is reached). In almost all circumstances, however, none of those three most common ages will give you the maximum lifetime benefit.

Remember, every month you wait to file, the amount of your benefit check goes up, but you also get one less check. You don't know how exactly how long you're going to live, but you have a better idea of your life expectancy than the actuaries at the Social Security Administration who can only work with averages. They can't make calculations based on your specific situation. A professional can run the numbers for you and get the target date that maximizes your potential lifetime benefits. You can't get this information from the SSA, but you *can* get it from a financial professional.

Your Social Security options don't stop here, however. There are a plethora of other choices you can make to manipulate your benefit payments.

Just a Few Types of Social Security Benefits.

Retired Worker Benefit. This is the benefit with which most people are familiar. The Retired Worker Benefit is what most people are talking about when they refer to Social Security. It is your benefit based on your earnings and the amount that you have paid into the system over the span of your career.

Spousal Benefit. The Spousal Benefit is available to the spouse of someone who is eligible for Retired Worker Benefits. What if there was a way for your spouse to receive his or her benefit for four years and not lose the chance to get his or her maximum benefit when he or she turns age 70? Many people do not know about this strategy and might be missing out on benefits they have earned.

Survivorship Benefit. When one spouse passes away, the survivor is able to receive the larger of the two benefit amounts.

File and Suspend. This concept allows for a lower-earning spouse to receive up to 50 percent of the other's PIA amount if both spouses file for benefits at the right time.

Restricted Application. A higher-earning spouse may be able to start collecting a spousal benefit on the lower-earning spouse's benefit while allowing his or her benefit to continue to grow.

THE DIVORCE FACTOR

How does a divorced spouse qualify for benefits? If you have gone through a divorce, it might affect the retirement benefit to which you are entitled.

A person can receive benefits as a divorced spouse on a former spouse's Social Security record if he or she:

- Was married to the former spouse for at least 10 years;
- Is at least age 62 years old;
- Is unmarried; and
- Is not entitled to a higher Social Security benefit on his or her own record.*

---

*http://www.ssa.gov/retire2/yourdivspouse.htm

With all of the different options, strategies and benefits to choose from, you can see why filing for Social Security is more complicated than just mailing in the paperwork. Gathering the data and making yourself aware of all your different options isn't enough to know exactly what to do, however. On the one hand, you can knock yourself out trying to figure out which options are best for you and wondering if you made the best decision. On the other hand, you can work with a financial professional who uses customized software that takes all the variables of your specific situation into account and calculates your best option.

You have tens of thousands of different options for filing for your Social Security benefit. If your spouse is a different age than you are, it nearly doubles the amount of options you have. This is far more complicated arithmetic than most people can do on their own. If you want a truly accurate understanding of when and how to file, you need someone who will ask you the right questions about your situation, someone who has access to specialized software that can crunch the numbers. The reality is that you need to work with a professional that can provide you with the sophisticated analysis of your situation that will help you make a truly informed decision.

Important Questions about Your Social Security Benefit:

- How can I maximize my lifetime benefit? By knowing when and how to file for Social Security. This usually means waiting until you have at least reached your Full Retirement Age. A professional has the experience and the tools to help determine when and how you can maximize your lifetime benefits.
- Who will provide reliable advice for making these decisions? Only a professional has the tools and experience to provide you reliable advice.

- Will the Social Security Administration provide me with the advice? The Social Security Administration cannot provide you with advice or strategies for claiming your benefit. They can give you information about your monthly benefit, but that's it. They also don't have the tools to tell you what your specific best option is. They can accurately answer how the system works, but they can't advise you on what decision to make as to how and when to file for benefits.

The Maximization Report that your financial professional will generate represents an invaluable resource for understanding how and when to file for your Social Security benefit. When you get your customized Social Security Maximization Report, you will not only know all the options available to you – but you will understand the financial implications of each choice. In addition to the analysis, you will also get a report that shows *exactly* at what age – including which month and year – you should trigger benefits and how you should apply. It also includes a variety of other time-specific recommendations, such as when to apply for Medicare or take Required Minimum Distributions from your qualified plans. A report means there is no need to wonder, or to try to figure out when to take action – the Social Security Maximization Report lays it all out for you in plain English.

CHAPTER 3 RECAP //

- To get the most out of your Social Security benefit, you need to file at the right time.
- An Investment Advisor can help you determine when you should file for Social Security to get your Maximum Lifetime Benefit.
- You have *I Need Now Money* needs and *I Need Later Money* needs. Creating an income plan is the first step toward providing for both of these needs.
- Maximizing your Social Security benefit depends on *when* and *how* you file so you'll need to examine your specific situation to find the best option for you.
- It's not impossible for you to calculate when the opportune time would be to trigger your Social Security income. In fact, with the tools and advice of a financial professional, it's quite easy.
- Every dollar your Social Security income increases is less money you'll have to spend from your nest egg to supplement your income.
- Your Social Security benefit is subject to taxes.
- Once you file for your benefit, you are permanently locked into that amount so be confident in your decision before you mail in your forms.

4

MAKING "A PLAN" INTO "*YOUR* PLAN"

Recall that the moment that you stop working and start living off the money that you've set aside for retirement can be referred to as the Retirement Cliff. You've worked and earned money your whole life, but the day that you retire, that working income comes to an end. That's the day that you have to have other assets that fill the gap. Social Security will fill in some, but you need to come up with something else. After you have calculated your Social Security benefit and have selected the year and month that will maximize your lifetime benefits, it's time to look at your other retirement assets, incomes and options that will reduce or eliminate the drop-off of the Retirement Cliff. You may have a pension, an IRA or Roth IRA, dividends from stock holdings, money from the sale of real estate, rental property, or other sources of income. What other sources of reliable income do you have?

If your monthly Social Security check and your other supplemental income leaves a shortfall in your *desired* income, how are you going to fix it? This shortfall is called the **Income Gap** and it needs to be filled in order to maintain your lifestyle into retirement. If you have a known income gap that you need to fill, you want to know how to fill that income gap with the fewest dollars possible. You basically want to buy that income gap for the least amount of money possible. You don't want it to cost you too much, because you want to get the most out of your other assets, including planning for your future and planning for your legacy. You do that by maximizing your Social Security benefit, leveraging your additional income, and looking at other investment tools that can help generate income for you. Your specific needs, of course, should be analyzed and consulted by a professional.

Today, you probably have savings in a variety of assets that you have acquired over the years, but you may not have taken time to examine them and assess how they will support your retirement. This is a vital examination to conduct because it's not about whether the market goes up or down, but *when* it does. If it goes down at the wrong time for your five or 10 year retirement horizon, you could be in serious danger of losing some of your retirement income.

Creating an income plan before you retire allows you to satisfy your need for lifetime income and ensures that your lifestyle can last as long as you do. You also want to create a plan that operates in the most efficient way possible. Doing so will give more security to your Need Later Money and will potentially allow you to build your legacy down the road.

» *Catherine wants to retire at age 69. However, after her Social Security benefit, she will need nearly $375,000 in assets to generate a modest $40,000 of income per year. Catherine is shocked: she never thought she'd need this much money to generate such a basic lifestyle. She's not sure how she can* *compensate for this shortfall. While having lunch with her daughter, Catherine mentions her predicament and wishes out loud that it was possible to put more money into Social Security so you could get more out of it and secure a guaranteed income. What an incredible Green Money asset that would be for her retirement! Catherine's daughter explains that there are financial vehicles that offer similar benefits as Social Security, and they can even come with more flexibility, and they're called annuities.*

IS AN ANNUITY RIGHT FOR YOU?

An annuity is a financial tool that is similar to Social Security in that it provides you with a reliable income. Moreover, an annuity has the potential to increase the value of your principal investment. If you have assets that you would like to structure for retirement income, ***an annuity may be the right choice for you.***

Consider the following questions:

- How concerned are you about finding a secure financial vehicle to protect your savings?
- How concerned are you that there may be a better way to structure your savings?

If these concerns are a top priority for you, an income annuity investment tool would likely be an invaluable component of your plan. Income annuities have many similar qualities to Social Security that give them the same look and feel as that reliable benefit check you get every month. Most importantly, an income annuity can be an efficient and profitable way to solve your income gap.

HOW ANNUITIES FIT INTO AN OVERALL INCOME PLAN

The term "annuity" may sound technical and unfamiliar, but it's an old concept with which you are very much familiar. Essentially, an "annuity" is just a way to invest your money that allows you to structure it for income. For example, a Social Security benefit and a pension are both basic forms of an annuity. Annuities come in a variety of different modes, touting a diverse array of features and benefits. One of the most seductive advantages of an annuity is that it provides a place to invest your money so it can at least keep pace with inflation and also be protected from market volatility. Finding the right one for you will take a conversation with your financial professional. Be sure you fully understand the features, benefits and costs of any annuity you are considering before investing money.

When you put your money into an annuity, you are essentially buying an investment product from an insurance company. It is a contract between you and the insurance company that provides the investment tool. Let's say you have saved $100,000 and need it to generate income to meet your needs above and beyond your Social Security and pension checks. You give the $100,000 to an insurance company, who in turn invests it to generate growth. They usually select investments that have modest returns over long term horizons. In other words, they generally put it somewhere stable and predictable. Most commonly, they will invest it in a combination of bonds and treasuries that are safer and dependable ways to grow money. They use the money from the insurance products they sell to invest, use a portion of the returns to generate profits for themselves, and return a portion to clients in the form of payouts, claims, and structured income options.

One of the most attractive qualities of these types of annuities is something called annual reset. Annual reset is sometimes also referred to as a "ratcheting." Instead of taking on the risk that comes with putting money in a fluctuating market, you can offset that risk onto the insurance company. It works like this: If the market goes down, you don't suffer a loss. Instead, the insurance company absorbs it. But if the market goes up, you share with the insurance company some of the profit made on the gain. The amount of gain you get is called your annuity participation rate. Typically the insurer will cap the amount of gain you can realize at somewhere between 3 and 7 percent. If the market goes up 10 percent, you would realize a portion of that gain (whatever percentage you are capped at). This means you avoid market downswings on your investment, while always gaining a portion of the upswings. The measurement period of your annuity can be calculated monthly, weekly and even daily, but most annuities are measured annually. The level of the index when you buy and the index level one year later will determine the amount of loss or gain. You and the insurance company are betting that the market will generally go up over time.

GETTING THE MOST OUT OF YOUR RIDE(R)

Keep in mind that annuities are, at their core, insurance products, which means that just like you can purchase additional coverage for your auto or homeowner's insurance policy to better make it suit your needs, you can do the same thing with an annuity. The additional benefit that you purchase separately from the base policy is what the term "rider" refers to. An income rider is probably the most common way to customize an annuity. Let's continue on with our example to see how it can work:

When you use that $100,000 to buy a contract with an insurance company in the form of an annuity, you are pegging your money on an index. It could be the S&P 500, the Dow Jones Industrial Average or any number of indexes. To generate income from the annuity, you select something called an income rider. An income rider is a subset of an indexed annuity. Essentially, it is the amount of money from which the insurance company will pay you an income while you have your money in their annuity. Your income rider is a larger number than what your investment is actually worth, and if you select the income rider, it will increase in value over time, providing you with more income. As the insurance company holds your money and invests it, they generate a return on it that they use to pay you a regular monthly income based on a higher number. The insurance company has to outperform the amount that they pay you in order to make a profit.

Remember, insurance companies make long-term investments that provide them with predictable flows of money. They like to stabilize the amount of money that goes in and out of their doors instead of paying and receiving large unpredictable chunks at once. When you opt for an income rider, an insurance company can reliably predict how much money they will pay out to you over a set period of time. It's predictable, and they like that. They can base their business on those predictable numbers.

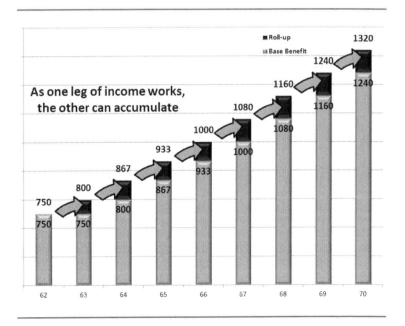

F

In order to encourage investors to leave their money in their annuity contracts, insurance companies create surrender periods that protect their investments. If you remove your money from the annuity contract during the surrender period, you will pay a penalty and will not be able to receive your entire investment amount back. A typical surrender period is 10 years. If after three years you decide that you want your $100,000 back, the insurance company has that money tied up in bonds and other investments with the understanding that they will have it for another seven years. Because they will take a hit on removing the money from their investments prematurely, you will have to pay a surrender charge that makes up for their loss. During the surrender period, an annuity is not a demand deposit account like a savings or checking account. The higher returns that you are guaranteed from an annuity are dependent on the timeframe you selected. The longer an insurance company can hold your money, the easier it is for them to guarantee a predictable return on it.

If you leave your money in the annuity contract, you get a reliable monthly income no matter what happens in the market. Once the surrender period has expired, you can remove your money whenever you want. Your money becomes liquid again because the insurance company has used it in an investment that fit the timeline of your surrender period. For many people, this is an attractive trade off that can provide a creative solution for filling their income gap.

When is an annuity with an income rider right for you? A good financial professional can help you make that determination by taking the time to listen closely to your situation and understanding what your needs are as you enter retirement. Additionally a financial professional can help you make a selection from the many other riders you can use to modify an annuity to make it function more purposefully within your retirement plan. A Death Benefit Rider is incredibly useful if you want to use your annuity as a legacy-planning tool in addition to its role as an income-planning tool.

Essentially, a Death Benefit Rider allows you to select a beneficiary for your annuity. Some Death Benefit Riders will also allow you to guarantee the amount an annuity will payout to a beneficiary. Moreover, a critical care rider can be used to help offset costs associated with healthcare. This can be a particularly useful option for individuals who either can't afford a long-term healthcare option or who were not able to qualify because of their health.

Every salesperson has a bag full of brochures and PowerPoint presentations, but they need to know exactly what the financial concerns of their individual clients are in order to help them make the most informed and beneficial decision. Some people need income today; others need it in five or 10 years. Others may have their income needs met but are planning to move closer to their children and will need to buy a house in 10 years. Or, if you want income in 15 years, you might want to choose a different investment product for 10 years, and then switch to an annuity with an income rider during the last five years of your timeline. Everyone's situation is different and everyone's needs are different. An annuity is an excellent tool to use for people interested in designing a distinctively personalized retirement plan because they are flexible and capable of producing a guaranteed income stream, which will help you better secure your and your family's future. Talking to a financial professional is the best way to find out which annuity need and if you need to use a rider to provide you with additional coverage.

THE ANNUITY RIGHT FOR YOU

There are several different kinds of annuities to choose from depending on the requirements of your financial circumstance and your risk tolerance:

Fixed Annuities pay guaranteed rates of interest, which makes them function almost like a Certificate of Deposit (CD) except that they pay out at a higher rate. For example, a fixed five year annuity is paying at a tax deferred rate of about 3.5 percent. Essentially, fixed annuities are a good way to "beat the bank" without risking your principal investment.

Fixed Index Annuities increase at rates determined by the market: if the market does well, a fixed index annuity may result in higher yields than either a CD or a fixed annuity. While fixed index annuities rates of growth are linked to the market, this does not mean fixed index annuities *vary* with the market because if the market does poorly you do not suffer a loss to your principal. By attaching an income rider, this can provide lifelong guaranteed income.

Variable Annuities, however, do vary with the market, which means they can lose money according to market fluctuations. These annuities do not take advantage of annual reset when the market goes down. The income rider will stay the same, but the value of your actual contract may fall. If you surrender the annuity, the insurance company will pay you the market value of the asset, regardless of whether it matches, exceeds or falls short of the value at which you bought the contract. If its value has dropped significantly, you may be better off taking the income rider without surrendering your contract. Essentially, this type of annuity acts like a bunch of mutual funds that are tax-deferred. Be aware that this annuity can be quite risky and may not be advisable for investors who are drawn to annuities for their income generating capabilities.

Single Premium Immediate Annuities (SPIA) are structured so that you pay a lump sum of money (a single premium) to an insurance company, and they immediately begin giving you a guaranteed income over an agreed upon time period, which could be as short as five years or as long as the remainder of your lifetime. SPIAs provide investors with a stream of reliable income when they can't afford to take the risk of losing money in a fluctuating market. While there is general faith that the market always trends up, at least in the long-term, if you are focusing on income over a shorter period of time, you may not be able to take a big hit in the market. Beyond normal market volatility, interest rates also come with an inherent level of uncertainty, making it hard to create a dependable income on your own. SPIAs reduce risk for you by giving you regular monthly, quarterly or yearly payments that can begin the moment you buy the contract.

ANNUITIES IN ACTION

Ultimately, annuities are investment tools that look and feel a bit like Social Security: every year you allow the money to grow with the market, and it will "roll up" by a specific amount, paying out a specific percent to you as income each year. They are versatile financial vehicles that can be used to better customize your retirement plan. Just like with any investment strategy, however, be sure that your annuity is fulfilling a specific purpose and falls within your risk tolerance. Here are some general ways to manage risk within your annuity:

If you want to structure an annuity investment for growth over a long period of time, you can select a variable annuity. The value of your principal investment follows the market and can lose or gain value with the market. This type of annuity can also have an income rider, but it is really more useful as an accumulation tool that bets on an improving market. A 40-year-old couple, for example, will probably want to structure more for growth and take on more risk than someone in their 70s. The 40-year-old couple may select a variable annuity with an income rider that kicks in when they plan to retire. If it rises with the market or outperforms it, the value of their investment has grown. If the market loses ground over the duration of the contract or their annuity underperforms, they can still rely on the income rider.

If you are 68 years old and you have more immediate income needs that you need to come up with above and beyond your Social Security, you need a low risk, reliable source of income. If you choose an annuity option, you are looking for something that will pay out an income right away over a relatively short timeframe. You probably want to opt for a SPIA that pays you immediately and spans a five year period, as well as an additional annuity that begins paying you in five years, and another longer term annuity that begins paying you in 10 years. Bear in mind that each annuity contract has its own costs and fees. Review these with your financial professional before you determine the best products and strategies for your situation.

The following example shows just how helpful an indexed annuity option can be for a retiree:

> » Darla and Parker are 62 years old and have decided to run the numbers to see what their retirement is going to look like. They know they currently need $6,000 per month to pay their bills and maintain their current lifestyle. They have also done their Social Security homework and have determined that, between the two of them, they will receive $4,200 per month in benefits. They also receive $350 per month in rent from a tenant who lives in a small carriage house in their backyard. Between their Social Security and the monthly rent income, they will be short $1,450 per month.
>
> They do have an additional asset, however. They have been contributing for years to IRAs that has reached a value of $350,000. They realize that they have to figure out how to turn the $350,000 in their IRAs into $1,450 per month for the rest of their life. At first glance, it may seem like they will have plenty of money. With some quick calculations, they find they have 240 months, or nearly 20 years, of monthly income before they exhaust their accounts. When you consider income tax, the potential for higher taxes in the future, and market fluctuations (because many IRAs are invested in the market),

the amount in the IRAs seems to have a little less clout. Every dollar Parker and Darla take out of their IRAs is subject to income tax, and if they leave the remainder in their IRAs, they run the risk of losing money in a volatile market. Once they retire and stop getting a paycheck every two weeks, they also stop contributing to their IRAs. And when they aren't supplementing its growth with their own money, they are entirely dependent on market growth. That's a scary prospect. They could also withdraw the money from their IRAs and put it in a savings account or CD, but removing all the money at once will put them in a tax bracket that will claim a huge portion of the value of their IRAs. A seemingly straightforward asset has now become a complicated equation. Darla and Parker didn't know what to do, so they met with their financial professional.

Their financial professional suggested that they use the money to purchase an indexed annuity with an income rider. They selected an annuity that was designed for their specific situation. They transferred the lump sums from their IRAs, placed it in an indexed annuity taking advantage of annual reset so they never lost the value of their investment. In return, they were guaranteed the $1,450 of income per month that they needed to meet their retirement goals. The simplicity of the contract allowed them to do an analysis with their professional just once to understand the product. They basically put their money in an investment crockpot where they didn't have to look at it or manage it. They just needed to let it simmer. In fact, their professional was able to find an annuity for them that allowed them their $1,450 monthly payment with a lump sum of $249,455, leaving them more than $100,000 to reinvest somewhere else. Keep in mind that annuities are tax deferred, meaning you will pay tax on the income you receive from an annuity in the year you receive it.

» *Gabrielle is 60 years old and is wondering how she can use her assets to provide her with a retirement income. She has a $5,000 per month income need. If she starts withdrawing her Social Security benefit in six years at age 66, it will provide her with $2,200 per month. She also has a pension that kicks in at age 70 that will give her another $1,320 per month.*

That leaves an income gap of $2,800 from ages 66 to 69, and then an income gap of $1,480 at age 70 and beyond. If Gabrielle uses only Green Money to solve her income need, she will need to deposit $918,360 at 2 percent interest to meet her monthly goal for her lifetime. If she opts to use Red Money and withdraws the amount she needs each month from the market, let's say the S & P 500, she would have run out of cash in 10 years if she had invested between the years of 2000 and 2012. Suffering a market downturn like that during the period for which she is relying on it for retirement income will change her life, and not for the better.

Working with a financial professional to find a better way, Gabrielle found that she could take a hybrid approach to fill her income gap. Her professional recommended two different income vehicles: one that allowed her to deposit just $190,161 with a 2 percent return, and one that was a $146,000 income annuity. These tools filled her income gap with $336,161, requiring her to spend $582,000 less money to accomplish her goal! Working with a professional to find the right tools for her retirement needs saved Gabrielle over half a million dollars.

As you can see from the above examples, utilizing an annuity within your plan can be the perfect way to make your retirement plan function more comprehensively and purposefully. Moving forward, keep this basic roadmap of what we have covered so far in mind:

Review your income needs and look specifically at the shortfall you may have during each year of your retirement based on your Social Security income, and income from any other assets you have. Ask yourself where you are in your distribution phase. Is retirement one year away? 10 years away? Last year?

Determine how much money you need and how you need to structure your existing assets to provide for that need.

If you have an asset from which you need to generate income, consider options offered by purchasing an income rider on an annuity.

CHAPTER 4 RECAP //

- After Social Security and your additional income is accounted for, the amount that's left to meet your needs is called the *Income Gap.*
- Having an income plan will help you get a picture of what your retirement is really going to look like.
- Integrating your Social Security options with the rest of your income plan will give you an idea of how much more money you need.
- It is important to find ways to leverage your retirement assets to satisfy your need for lifetime income.
- An annuity may be a good way to fill your income gap because it can provide you with a guaranteed income source and it has growth potential with little to no risk exposure.
- Be sure you understand the features, benefits, costs and fees associated with any annuity product before you invest.

5

WHAT IS YELLOW MONEY?

Understanding your Social Security benefit, filling the income gap and making an overall plan that meets your retirement income needs is no small task. Once you have worked with a financial professional to structure your income needs, it's time to take a look at the future. With your immediate income needs met, you have the opportunity to take your additional assets and leverage them for profit to supplement your income in the future, to prepare for anticipated health care costs or to contribute to your legacy. Stable income also means that you should have the staying power to stick with your investment portfolio through the ups and downs in the market.

Now that you've calculated the Rule of 100, determined how much risk you have and how much you want, and you've determined how much Green Money you need to meet your short-term and mid-term income needs, it's time to look at what you have left. The money you have left after you've calculated your

Green Money needs has the potential of becoming Red Money: your stocks, mutual funds and other investment products that you want to continue accumulating value with the market. You now have the luxury of taking a closer second look at your Red Money to determine how you would like to manage it.

A FAIR-WEATHER FRIEND

A fickle market can raise the eyebrows of even the most veteran investor. For an individual who is invested in the market, however, that statement becomes even more true. Taking a hit in the market hurts no matter how stable your income. Part of the pain comes from knowing that when you take a step back in the market, it requires an even larger step forward to return to where you were. As the market goes up and down, those larger gains you need to realize to get back to zero start to look even more daunting.

It can be challenging to watch the stock market's erratic changes every month, week or even every day. When you have your money riding on it, the ride can feel pretty bumpy. When you are managing your money by yourself, emotions inevitably enter into the mix. The Dow Jones Industrial Average and the S&P 500 represent more to you than market fluctuations. They represent a portion of your retirement. It's hard not to be emotional about it.

Everyone knows you should buy low and sell high. But this is what is more likely to happen:

The market takes a downturn, similar to the 2008 crash, and investors see as much as a 30 percent loss in their stock holdings. It's hard to watch, and it's harder to bear the pain of losing that much money. The math of rebounds means that they will need to rely on even larger gains just to get back to where things were before the downturn. They sell. But eventually, and inevitably, the market begins to rise again. Maybe slowly, maybe with some moderate growth, but by the time the average investor notices an upward trend and wants to buy in again, they have already missed a great deal of the gains.

YELLOW MONEY

So, we know that some of our money has to be Red Money, which begs the question: how much of your Red Money do you invest, and in what kinds of markets, investment products and stocks do you invest? There are a lot of different directions in which you can take your Red Money. One thing is for sure: significant accumulation depends on investing in the market. How you go about doing it is different for everyone. Gathering stocks, bonds and investment funds together in a portfolio without a cohesive strategy behind them could cause you to miss out on the benefits of a more thoughtful and simple approach. The end result is that you may never really understand what your money is doing, where and how it is really invested, and which investment principles are behind the investment products you hold. While you may have goals for each individual piece of your portfolio, it is likely that you don't have a comprehensive plan for your Red Money, which may mean that *you are taking on more risk than you would like, and are getting less return for it than is possible.*

Enter **Yellow Money.** Yellow Money is money that is managed by a professional *with a purpose.* After your income needs are met and you have assets that you would like to dedicate to accumulation, there are decisions you need to make about how to invest those assets. You can buy stocks, index funds, mutual funds, bonds — you name it — you can invest in it. However, the difference between Red Money and Yellow Money is that Yellow Money has a cohesive strategy behind it that is *implemented by a professional.* When you manage your Red Money with an investment plan, it becomes Yellow Money: *money that is being managed with a specific purpose, a specific set of focused goals and a specific strategy in mind.* Yellow Money is still a type of Red Money. It comes with different levels of risk. But Yellow Money is under the watchful eye of professionals who have a stake in the success of your money in the market and who can recommend a range of strategies from those designed for preservation to those targeting rapid growth. You don't want to miss out on achieving the right level of risk, and more importantly, composing a careful plan for the return of your assets.

Yellow Money is generally I Need Later Money that you want to grow for needs you'll have in at least 10 years. You can work with your financial planner to create investments that meet your needs within different timeframes. You may need to rely on some of your Yellow Money in 10, 15 or 20 years, whether for additional income, a large purchase you plan on making or a vacation. Whatever you want it for, you will need it down the road. A financial professional can help you rescale the risk of your assets as they grow, helping you lock in your profits and secure a source of income you can depend on later.

VOLATILITY AND THE INDIVIDUAL INVESTOR

To understand the importance of Yellow Money, let's take a closer look at the impact of volatility on the individual investor:

> » *Mariana's situation illustrates how market volatility can have major repercussions for an individual investor. Mariana worked for Delta Pen Company for 30 years. During her time there, she received bonuses and pay raises that often included shares of stock in the company. She also dedicated part of her paycheck every month to a 401(k) that bought Delta stock. By the time she retired, Mariana had accumulated $250,000 worth of Acme stock.*
>
> *Although she had contributed to her 401(k) account every month, Mariana didn't cultivate any other assets that could generate income for her during retirement. Mariana also retired early at age 62 because of her failing health. The commute to*

work every day was too difficult in her weakened condition and she wanted to enjoy the rest of her life in retirement instead of continuing to work at Acme.

Because she retired early, Mariana failed to maximize her Social Security benefit. While she lives a modest lifestyle, her income needs are still $3,500 per month. Mariana's monthly Social Security check only covers $1,900, leaving her with a $1,600 income gap. To supplement her Social Security check, Mariana has to sell $1,600 of her Delta stock each month to meet her income needs. A $250,000 401(k) is nothing to sneeze at, but reducing its value by $1,600 every month will barely last Mariana 10 years. And that's if the market stays neutral or grows modestly. If the market takes a downturn, the money that Mariana is relying on to fill her income gap will rapidly diminish. Even if the market starts going up in a couple of years, it will take much larger gains for her to recover the value that she lost.

Unhappily for Mariana, she retired in 2007, just before the major market downturn that lasted for several years. She lost more than 20 percent of the value of her stock. Because Mariana needed to sell her stock to meet her basic income needs, the market price of the stock was secondary to her need for the money. When she needed money, she was forced to sell however many shares she needed to fill her income gap that month. And if she has a financial crisis, involving her need for medical care, for example, she will be forced to sell stock even if the market is low and her shares are nearly worthless.

Mariana now realizes that she could have relied on an investment structured to deliver her a regular income while protecting the value of her investment. She could have kept her $250,000 from diminishing while enjoying her lifestyle into retirement regardless of the volatility of the market. Ideally, Mariana would have restructured her 401(k) to reflect the

*level of risk that she was able to take. In her case, she would
have had most of her money in Green Money assets, allowing
her to rely on the value of her assets when she needed them.*

In 2013, DALBAR, the well-respected financial services market
research firm, released their annual "Quantitative Analysis of
Investment Behavior" report (QAIB). The report studied the impact
of market volatility on individual investors: people like Mariana, or
anyone who was managing (or mismanaging) their own investments
in the stock market.

According to the study, volatility not only caused investors
to make decisions based on their emotions, those decisions also
harmed their investments and prevented them from realizing
potential gains. So why do people meddle so much with their
investments when the market is fluctuating? Part of the reason
is that many people have financial obligations that they don't
have control over. Significant expenses like house payments, the
unexpected cost of replacing a broken-down car, and medical bills
can put people in a position where they need money. If they need
to sell investments to come up with that money, they don't have
the luxury of selling when they *want* to. They must sell when they
need to.

DALBAR's "Quantitative Analysis of Investor Behavior" has
been used to measure the effects of investors' buying, selling and
mutual fund switching decisions since 1994. The QAIB shows time
and time again over nearly a 20 year period that the average investor
earns less, and in many cases, significantly less than the performance
of mutual funds suggests. QAIB's goal is to improve independent
investor performance and to help financial professionals provide
helpful advice and investment strategies that address the concerns
and behaviors of the average investor.

An excerpt from the report claims that:

"QAIB offers guidance on how and where investor behaviors can be improved. No matter what the state of the mutual fund industry, boom or bust: Investment results are more dependent on investor behavior than on fund performance. Mutual fund investors who hold on to their investments are more successful than those who time the market.

QAIB uses data from the Investment Company Institute (ICI), Standard & Poor's and Barclays

There are actually three primary causes for the chronic shortfall for both equity and fixed income investors:

- *Capital not available to invest. This accounts for 25 percent to 35 percent of the shortfall.*
- *Capital needed for other purposes. This accounts for 35 percent to 45 percent of the shortfall.*
- *Psychological factors. These account for 45 percent to 55 percent of the shortfall."*

The key findings of Dalbar's QAIB report provide compelling statistics about how individual investment strategies produced negative outcomes for the majority of investors:

- Psychological factors account for 45 percent to 55 percent of the chronic investment return shortfall for both equity and fixed income investors.
- Asset allocation is designed to handle the investment decision-making for the investor, which can materially reduce the shortfall due to psychological factors.
- Successful asset allocation investing requires investors to act on two critical imperatives:
- Balance capital preservation and appreciation so that they are aligned with the investor's objective.
- Select a qualified allocator.
- The best way for an investor to determine their risk tolerance is to utilize a risk tolerance assessment. However, these assessments must be accessible and usable.

- Evaluating allocator quality requires analysis of the allocator's underlying investments, decision making process and whether or not past efforts have produced successful outcomes.
- Choosing a top allocator makes a significant difference in the investment results one will achieve.
- Mutual fund retention rates suggest that the average investor has not remained invested for long enough periods to derive the potential benefits of the investment markets.
- Retention rates for asset allocation funds exceed those of equity and fixed income funds by over a year.
- Investors' ability to correctly time the market is highly dependent on the direction of the market. Investors generally guess right more often in up markets. However, in 2012 investors guessed right only 42 percent of the time during a bull market.
- Analysis of investor fund flows compared to market performance further supports the argument that investors are unsuccessful at timing the market. Market upswings rarely coincide with mutual fund inflows while market downturns do not coincide with mutual fund outflows.
- Average equity mutual fund investors gained 15.56 percent compared to a gain of 15.98 percent that just holding the S&P 500 produced.
- The shortfall in the long-term annualized return of the average mutual fund equity investor and the S&P 500 continued to decrease in 2012.
- The fixed-income investor experienced a return of 4.68 percent compared to an advance of 4.21 percent on the Barclays Aggregate Bond Index.
- The average fixed income investor has failed to keep up with inflation in nine out of the last 14 years.*

*2013 QAIB, Dalbar, March 2013

It doesn't take a financial services market research report to tell you that market volatility is out of your control. The report does prove, however, that before you experience market volatility, you should have an investment plan, and when the market is fluctuating, you should stand by your investment plan. You should also review and discuss your investment plan with your financial professional on a regular basis, ensuring he/she is aware of any changes in your goals, financial circumstances, your health or your risk tolerance.

When the economy is under stress and the markets are volatile, investors can feel vulnerable. That vulnerability causes people to tinker with their portfolios in an attempt to outsmart the market. Financial professionals, however, don't try to time the market for their clients. They try to tap into the gains that can be realized by committing to long-term investment strategies.

As you can see, the deck is stacked against the individual investor. This is why Yellow Money is so important. It can be helpful to think of Red Money and Yellow Money with this analogy:

If you needed to travel through an unfamiliar city in a foreign country, you could rent a car or perhaps hire a driver. Were you to drive yourself, you would try to gain guidance from perplexing road signs and need to adhere to traffic rules – with no experience or assistance to lean on. It would take longer to get to where you want to go, and the chance of a traffic accident would be higher. If you hired a driver, they would manage your journey. A driver would know the route, how to avoid traffic, and follow the rules of the road.

Red Money is like driving yourself. With Yellow Money, you are still traveling by car, but now you have a professional working on your behalf.

YELLOW MONEY IN ACTION

Now that you understand the importance of Yellow Money, let's look at how you can take your Red Money and change its color. As you read earlier in the key findings of the DALBAR report, the deck is stacked against the individual investor. Remember that the average investor on a fixed income failed to keep pace with inflation in nine of the last 14 years, meaning the inherent risk in managing your Red Money is very real and could have a lasting impact on your assets.

TAKING A CLOSER LOOK AT YOUR PORTFOLIO

Think about your investment portfolio. Think specifically of what you would consider your Red Money. Do you know what is there? You may have several different investment products like individual mutual funds, bond accounts, stocks, etc. You may have inherited a stock portfolio from a relative, or you might be invested in a bond account offered by the company for which you worked due to your familiarity with them. While you may or may not be managing your investments individually, the reality is that you probably don't have an overall management strategy for all of your investments. Investments that aren't managed are simply Red Money, or money that is at risk in the market. Harnessing the earning potential of your Red Money relies on more than a collection of stocks and bonds, however. It needs guided management. A good Yellow Money manager uses the knowledge they have about the level of risk with which you are comfortable, what you need or want to use your money for, when you want it or need it and how you want to use it. The Yellow Money objects that they choose for you will still have a certain level of risk, but under the right management, control and process, you have a far better chance of a successful outcome that meets your specific needs.

When you sit down with an investment professional, you can look at all of your assets together. Chances are that you have accumulated a number of different assets over the last 20, 30 or 50 years. You may have a 401(k), an IRA, a Roth IRA, an account of self-directed stocks, a brokerage account, etc. Wherever you put your money, a financial professional will review your assets and help you determine the level of risk to which you are exposed now and should be exposed in the future.

Here is a typical example of how an investment professional can be helpful to a future retiree with Yellow Money needs:

> » *Denise is 65 years old and wants to retire in two years. She has a 401(k) from her job to which she has contributed for 26 years. She also has some stocks that her late husband managed. Denise also has $55,000 in a mutual fund that her sister recommended to her five years ago and $30,000 in another mutual fund that she heard about at work. She takes a look at her assets one day and decides that she doesn't understand what they add up to or what kind of retirement they will provide. She decides to meet with an investment professional.*
>
> *Denise's professional immediately asks her:*
>
> ***Does she know exactly where all of her money is?*** *Denise doesn't know much about all her husband's stocks, which have now become hers. Their value is at $100,000 invested in three large cap companies. Janet is unsure of the companies and whether she should hold or sell them.*
>
> ***Does she know what types of assets she owns?*** *Yes and no. She knows she had a 401(k) and an IRA, but she is unfamiliar with her husband's self-directed stock portfolio or the type of mutual funds she now owns. Furthermore she is unclear as to how to manage the holdings as she nears retirement.*
>
> ***Does she know the strategies behind each one of the investment products she owns?*** *While Denise knows she had a 401(k), an IRA and mutual fund holdings, she doesn't*

know how her 401(k) is organized or how to make it more conservative as she nears retirement. She is unsure whether her IRA is a Roth or traditional variety and how to draw income from them. She really does not have specific investment principles guiding her investment decisions, and she doesn't know anything about her husband's individual stocks. One major concern for Denise is whether her family would be okay if she were not around.

After determining Denise's assets, her financial professional prepares a consolidated report that lays out all of her assets for her to review. Her professional explains each one of them to her. Denise discovers that although she is two years away from retiring, her 401(k) is organized with an amount of risk with which she is not comfortable. Sixty percent of her 401(k) is at risk, far off the mark if we abide by the Rule of 100. Denise opts to be more conservative than the Rule of 100 suggests, as she will rely on her 401(k) for most of her immediate income needs after retirement. Denise's professional also points out several instances of overlap between her mutual funds. Denise learns that while she is comfortable with one of her mutual funds, she does not agree with the management principles of the other. In the end, Denise's professional helps her re-organize her 401(k) to secure her more Green Money for retirement income. Her professional also uses her mutual fund and her husband's stock assets to create a growth oriented investment plan that Janet will rely on for I Need Later Money in 15 years when she plans on relocating closer to her children and grandchildren. By creating an overall investment strategy, Janet is able to meet her targeted goals in retirement. Denise's financial professional worked closely with her and her tax professional to minimize the tax impact of any asset sales on Denise's situation.

Like Denise, you may have several savings vehicles: a 401(k), an IRA to which you regularly contribute, some mutual funds to which you make monthly contributions, etc. But what is your *overall investment strategy*? Do you have one in place? Do you want one that will help you meet your retirement goals? Yellow Money looks at *ALL* your accounts and all their different strategies to create a plan that helps them all work together. Your current investment situation may not reflect your wishes. As a matter of fact, it likely doesn't.

You may have a better understanding of your assets than Denise did, but even someone with an investment strategy can benefit from having a financial professional review their portfolio:

> » *Charles is 69 years old. He retired four years ago. He relied on income from an IRA for three years in order to increase his Social Security benefit. He also made significant investments in 36 different mutual funds. He chose to diversify among the funds by selecting a portion for growth, another for good dividends, another that focused on promising small cap companies and a final portion that work like index funds. All the money that Charles had in mutual funds he considered Need Later Money that he wanted to rely on in his 80s. After the stock market took a hit in 2008, Charles lost some confidence in his investments and decided to sit down with a financial professional to see if his portfolio was able to recover.*
>
> *The professional Charles met with was able to determine what goals he had in mind. Specifically, the financial professional determined what Charles actually wanted and needed the money for, and when he needed it. His professional also looked inside each of the mutual funds and discovered several instances of overlap. While Charles had created diversity in his portfolio by selecting funds focused on different goals, he didn't account for overlap in the companies in which the funds*

were invested. Out of the 36 funds, his professional found that 20 owned nearly identical stock. While most of the companies were good investments, the high instance of overlap did not contribute to the healthy investment diversity that Charles wanted. Charles's financial professional also provided him with a report that explained the concentration ratio of his holdings (noting how much of his portfolio was contained within the top 25 stock holdings), the percentage of his portfolio that each company in which he invested in represented (showing the percentage of net assets that each company made up as an overall position in his portfolio) and the portfolio date of his account (showing when the funds in his portfolio were last updated: as funds are required to report updates only twice per year, it was possible that some of his fund reports could be six months old).

Charles's professional consolidated his assets into one investment management strategy. This allowed Charles's investments to be managed by someone he trusted who knew his specific investment goals and needs. Eliminating redundancy and overlap in his portfolio was easy to do but difficult to detect since Charles had multiple funds with multiple brokerage firms. Charles sat down with a professional to see if his mutual funds could perform well, and he left with a consolidated management plan and a money manager that understood him personally. That's Yellow Money at its best.

AVOIDING EMOTIONAL INVESTING

As you've learned, it's a bad idea to emotionally invest but there's no way around it: people get emotional about their money. And understandably so! You've spent your life working for it, exchanging your time and talent for it, and making decisions about how to invest it, save it and make it grow. The maintenance of your lifestyle and your plans for retirement all depend on it. The best investment strategies, however, don't rely on emotions. One of Yellow Money's greatest strengths lies in the fact that it is managed by someone who understands your needs and desires, but doesn't make decisions about your money under the influence of emotion.

A well-managed investment account meets your goals as a whole, not in individualized and piecemeal ways. Professional money managers do this by creating requirements for each type of investment in which they put your money. We'll call them "screens." Your money manager will run your holdings through the screens they have created to evaluate different types of investment strategies. A professionally managed account will only have holdings that meet the requirements laid out in the overall management plan that was designed to meet your investment goals. The holdings that don't make it through the screens, the ones that don't contribute to your investment goals, can be sold and redistributed to investments that your financial professional has determined to be appropriate.

Different screens apply to different Yellow Money strategies. For example, if one of your goals is significant growth, which would require taking on more risk alongside the potential for more return, an investment professional would screen for companies that have high rates of revenue and sales growth, high earnings growth, rising profit margins, and innovative products. On the other hand, if you want your portfolio to be used for income, which would call for lower risk and less return, your professional would screen for dividend yield and sector diversification. *Every investor has a different goal, and every goal requires a customized strategy that uses quantitative screens.* A professional will create a portfolio that reflects your investment desires. If some of the current assets you own complement the strategies that your professional recommends, those will likely stay in your portfolio.

Screening your assets removes emotions from the equation. It removes attachment to underperforming or overly risky investments. Financial professionals aren't married to particular stocks or mutual funds for any reason. They go by the numbers and see your portfolio through a lens shaped by your retirement goals. Your professional understands your wants and needs, and creates an investment strategy that takes your life events and future plans into account. It's a simple approach, and it allows you to tap into the tools and resources of a professional who has built a career around successful investing. Managing money is a full time job and is best left to a professional money manager.

Removing emotions from investing also allows you to be unaffected by the day-to-day volatility of the market. Your financial professional doesn't ask where the market is going to be in a year, three years or a month from now. If you look at the value of the stock market from the beginning of the twentieth century to today, it's going up. Despite the Great Depression, despite the 1987 crash, despite the 2008 market downturn, the market, as a whole, trends up. Remember the major market downturn in 2008 when the market lost 30 percent of its value? Not only did it completely recover, it has far exceeded its 2008 value. Emotional investing led countless people to sell low as the market went down, and buy the same shares back when the market started to recover. That's an expensive way to do business. While you can't afford to lose money that you need in two, three or five years, your I Need Later Money has time to grow. The best way to do so is to make it Yellow.

CREATING AN INVESTMENT STRATEGY

Just like Denise and Charles, chances are that you can benefit from taking a more managed investment approach tailored to your goals.

So what does a Yellow Money account look like? Here's what it *doesn't* look like: a portfolio with 49 small cap mutual funds, a dozen individual stocks and an assortment of bond accounts. A brokerage account with a hodgepodge of investments, even if goal-oriented, is not a professionally managed account. It's still Red

Money. Remember, Yellow Money is a managed account that has an overarching investment philosophy. When you look at making investments that will perform to meet your future income needs, the burning question becomes: How much should you have in the market and how should it be invested? Working with a professional will help you determine how much risk you should take, how to balance your assets so they will meet your goals and how to plan for the big ticket items, like health care expenses, that may be in your future. Yes, Yellow Money is exposed to risk, but by working with a professional, you can manage that risk in a productive way.

WHY YELLOW MONEY?

If you have met your immediate income needs for retirement, why bother with professionally managing your other assets? The money you have accumulated above and beyond your income needs probably has a greater purpose. It may be for your children or grandchildren. You may want to give money to a charity or organization that you admire. In short, you may want to craft your legacy. It would be advantageous to grow your assets in the best manner possible. A financial professional has built a career around managing money in profitable ways. They are experts under the supervision of the organization that they represent.

Turning to Yellow Money also means that you don't have to burden yourself with the time commitment, the stress, and the cost of determining how to manage your money. Yellow Money can help you better enjoy your retirement. Do you want to sit down in your home office every day and determine how to best allocate your assets, or do you want to be living your life while someone else manages your money for you? When the majority of your Red Money is managed with a specific purpose by a financial professional, you don't have to be worrying about which stocks to buy and sell today or tomorrow.

SEEKING FINANCIAL ADVICE: STOCK BROKERS VS. INVESTMENT ADVISOR REPRESENTATIVES

Investors basically have access to two types of advice in today's financial world: advice from stock brokers and advice given by investment advisors. Most investors, however, don't know the difference between types of advice and the people from whom they receive advice. Today, there are two primary types of advice offered to investors: advice given by a commission-based registered representative (brokers) and advice given by fee-based Investment Advisor Representatives. Unfortunately, many investors are not aware that a difference exists; nor have they been explained the distinction between the two types of advice. In a survey taken in 2011 by TD Ameritrade, the top reasons investors choose to work with an independent registered investment advisor are:

- Registered Investment Advisors are required, as fiduciaries, to offer advice that is in the best interest of clients
- More personalized service and competitive fee structure offered at a Registered Investment Advisor firm
- Dissatisfaction with full commission brokers

The truth is that there is a great deal of difference between stock brokers and investment advisor representatives. For starters, investment advisor representatives are obligated to act in an investor's best interests in all aspects of a financial relationship. Confusion continues to exist among investors struggling to find the best financial advice out there and the most credible sources of advice.

Here is some information to help clear up the confusion so you can find good advice from a professional you can trust:

- Investment advisor representatives have the fiduciary duty to act in a client's best interest at all times with every investment decision they make. Stock brokers and brokerage firms usually do not act as fiduciaries to their investors and are not obligated to make decisions that are entirely in the best interest of their customers. For example, if you decide you want to invest in precious metals, a stock broker would offer you a precious metals account from their firm. An Investment Advisor would find you a precious metals account that is the best fit for you based on the investment strategy of your portfolio.

- Investment advisors give their clients a Form ADV describing the methods that the professional uses to do business. An Investment Advisor also obtains client consent regarding any conflicts of interest that could exist with the business of the professional.
- Stock brokers and brokerage firms are not obligated to provide comparable types of disclosure to their customers.
- Whereas stock brokers and firms routinely earn large profits by trading as principal with customers, Investment Advisors cannot trade with clients as principal (except in very limited and specific circumstances).
- Investment Advisors charge a pre-negotiated fee with their clients in advance of any transactions. They cannot earn additional profits or commissions from their customers' investments without prior consent. Registered Investment Advisors are commonly paid an asset-based fee that aligns their interests with those of their clients. Brokerage firms and stock brokers, on the other hand, have much different payment agreements. Their revenues may increase regardless of the performance of their customers' assets.
- Unlike brokerage firms, where investment banking and underwriting are commonplace, Registered Investment Advisors must manage money in the best interests of their customers. Because Registered Investment Advisors charge set fees for their services, their focus is on their client. Brokerage firms may focus on other aspects of the firm

that do not contribute to the improvement of their clients' assets.

- Unlike brokers, Registered Investment Advisors do not get commissions from fund or insurance companies for selling their investment products.

Just to drive home the point, here is what a fiduciary duty to a client means for a Registered Investment Advisor. Registered Investment Advisors must:*

- Always act in the best interest of their client and make investment decisions that reflect their goals.
- Identify and monitor securities that are illiquid.
- When appropriate, employ fair market valuation procedures.
- Observe procedures regarding the allocation of investment opportunities, including new issues and the aggregation of orders.
- Have policies regarding affiliated broker-dealers and maintenance of brokerage accounts.
- Disclose all conflicts of interest.
- Have policies on use of brokerage commissions for research.
- Have policies regarding directed brokerage, including step-out trades and payment for order flow.
- Abide by a code of ethics.

CHAPTER 5 RECAP //

- Yellow Money may make Red Money less dangerous.
- Yellow Money is professionally managed.
- Yellow Money has a cohesive purpose and a strategy behind it.

2011 Advisor Sentiment Study, commissioned by TD AMERITRADE. TD Ameritrade, Inc.

- If you haven't sat down and thought about how much money you need in order to generate income during retirement, you're just speculating.
- Red Money is like driving yourself in unfamiliar territory. With Yellow Money, you are still traveling by car, but now you have a professional driving on your behalf.
- The deck is stacked against the ordinary investor. According to the DALBAR report, individual investors consistently underperform compared to the market because of a variety of factors, including emotional investing.
- Yellow Money is managed without emotions.
- Checking your truly Red Money should be like checking the sports section. You are interested in it, but it won't directly affect your lifestyle. If your Red Money goes down 50 percent, no one should have to scrape you off the floor.

6

NEW IDEAS FOR INVESTING: INSURING YOUR PLAN AND YOUR FUTURE

It can be all too easy to only rely on traditional and outdated patterns of financial thinking but doing so results in retirement strategies that tend to be at best ineffective, and at worst downright destructive. The most familiar, and possibly most limiting, perspective to fall back on is framing investment through the old "risk versus reward" lens. With this viewpoint, investment opportunities are considered to exist solely along a sliding scale between risk and reward: the higher the exposure to volatility, the greater the return potential of the investment, while on the other hand, lower risk investments are accompanied by lower rates of return. For people who see all investments as the result of this trade-off, they often spend their financial lives sliding up and down this scale trying to strike a tolerable balance between risk and reward because according to this old investing rule, you can either choose relative safety *or* return, but you can't have both.

However, as you know by now, every financial product and strategy within a successful retirement plan is there because it serves a specific function and satisfies a specific need. In other words, there is no "one size fits all" when it comes to retirement planning because the most effective plan will be *your* plan: the one that has been carefully and purposefully crafted to meet the unique requirements of your situation. In order to do this in the most beneficial and effective way possible, you will need to use a financial perspective that is expansive enough to address your diverse needs and the limiting "risk versus reward" concept is too limiting to be it. However, by utilizing the flexibility of liquidity to rewrite the old investment rules, a broader financial scope is created, which will allow you to more creatively and advantageously address your retirement needs.

With this perspective, there are three dimensions that are inherent in any investment: *Liquidity, Safety,* and *Return.* You can maximize any two of these dimensions but at the expense of the third. For example, keeping all your assets in a checking account or savings account would provide a lot of Safety and Liquidity because your money would not be exposed to any market volatility and you would be able to access it whenever you wanted, but you would sacrifice any potential for Return because the money wouldn't be invested anywhere. Alternatively, if you chose Liquidity and Return as the two most important focal points of an investment, this decision would come at the expense of the investment's Safety so it would likely be exposed to a very high level of risk.

Understanding Liquidity can help you break the old Risk versus Safety trade-off. The sooner you want your money back, the less you can leverage it for Safety or Return. If you have the option of putting your money in a long-term investment, you will be sacrificing Liquidity, but potentially gaining both Safety and

Return. Ultimately, by identifying assets from which you don't require Liquidity, you can place yourself in a position to potentially profit from relatively safe investments that provide a higher than average rate of return.

LIQUIDITY AND RETIREMENT

Applying this three dimensional investment perspective can have profound effects when it comes to retirement planning, although it's more useful to think of Safety as preservation, Return as accumulation, and Liquidity as income. Just as it is a mistake to frame general investment decisions as being only a trade-off between Safety and Return, it is equally as problematic to frame retirement decisions as a trade-off between preservation and accumulation. As you've seen, your financial needs during retirement are complicated and satisfying them is not just a matter of figuring out an answer to the question, "how much money do I need to last my whole retirement and how can I acquire and protect it?" It's equally (if not more) important to answer the question of *when* you will need that money.

In other words, how much Liquidity do you *really* need? Think about it. If you haven't sat down and created an income plan for your retirement, your perceived need for Liquidity is a guess. You don't know how much cash you'll need to fill the income gap if you don't know the amount of your Social Security benefit or the total of your other income options. If you *have* determined your income need and have made a plan to fill your income gap, you can partition your assets based on when you will need them. Completing this exercise makes it much easier for you to see how you can apply new investment rules to get the most out of your assets, which is as important as ever thanks to economic forces beyond our control. When factors such as inflation, market volatility, increasing taxation, and fluctuating interest rates are taken into account, it becomes clear why successful retirement plans attempt to find the most profitable and practical balance between your preservation, accumulation, and income needs.

One of the hardest things about retirement planning is the financial mental shift it requires: the earning and saving paradigm that guided your financial life before retirement has to be replaced with an asset leveraging one. Utilizing the concept of Liquidity can help you prepare for this change. The shift will happen whether or not you're ready for it. In Ross's case, the transition from earning and saving to leveraging assets was a costly one.

> » *Ross is a citrus farmer with a little less than 2,000 acres of orange and grapefruit groves. Although Ross isn't an especially wealthy farmer, he generally has somewhere between $50,000 and $90,000 in his checking and savings account. However, this decision is the result of necessity and prudence, not frugality. Because of the extremely uncertain nature of his profession, Ross has to maintain a healthy "just in case fund." There are a lot of things that can go wrong for a farmer: a crucial piece of equipment could fail and need repair or replacement or the price of pesticides could increase significantly in any given year. In situations like these, Ross needs a substantial amount of money on-hand so he can quickly address the problem. For example, in the event of a mechanical failure of some sort Ross would need the money to fix or replace the machine right away so he would be able to continue farming. Likewise, if there was an unexpected increase in his overhead one year, he would need to have enough money available to make up the difference so he could carry on. Most of Ross's capital is tied up with the fruit in the trees and is thus unavailable for a portion of the year, which means that when a major financial need arises, Ross can't just go out to the orange grove and quickly pick a few hundred bushels or so and then use them for payment. Consequently, Ross always needs to have a substantial portion*

of money readily available because the survival of his business is dependent on his ability to quickly fix a problem. In order to be a successful farmer, he needs to depend heavily on Liquidity.

However, as the saying goes, you can't teach an old dog new tricks so even when Ross finally hangs up his shears and quits farming, he keeps his bank accounts as full as he can, just like he always has. After selling his groves and the equipment, Ross keeps a huge amount of the profits in Liquid investments because that's the only way he's ever done it. As a result, Ross has a big pile of money parked in his checking account and it isn't even keeping pace with inflation. After all his hard work as a farmer, the value of Ross's money decreases every day because he didn't shift to a financial paradigm based on leveraging his assets to generate income and accumulate value.

Almost anything would be a better option for Ross than clinging to Liquidity. He could have done something better to get either more return from his money or more safety, and at the very least would not have lost out to inflation.

Focusing solely on Liquidity is just one of the mistakes Ross made when it came to his retirement: not creating a comprehensive, purposeful, and easy to understand plan is another. Had Ross rethought his approach to money and had a better plan for retirement, he could have developed an investment strategy that would have helped him structure his assets in a way to both generate income and maintain some of their growth potential. As you know, there is no single investment tool or strategy that perfectly accomplishes this goal. However, having a broader investment perspective does allow you to consider options that might otherwise be overlooked: using life insurance is one such tool.

LIFE INSURANCE: MORE THAN MEETS THE EYE

Traditionally, life insurance is considered solely to be a legacy planning tool and not seen as an investment vehicle for building wealth and retirement planning. All too often, when people hear the term "life insurance," what they really hear is "death benefit," and this unfortunate misconception causes the other versatile and invaluable benefits of life insurance to be overlooked. While it's true that there is no better way than life insurance to continue to financially protect and support our loved ones even after we are gone, the truth of the matter is that it is also an incredibly diverse tool that can be used to serve a variety of different financial functions.

On the surface, purchasing a life insurance policy does accomplish exactly what it is most well-known for: it ensures that our loved ones will receive enough income from the insurance company to help them pay our final expenses and to comfortably carry on with their lives without us when we die. However, the true utility of a life insurance policy runs much deeper than this ability for three main reasons: first and foremost, any money paid out by a life insurance policy will not be taxed; secondly, many policies carry within them a cash accumulation value; and finally, you can receive money from your life insurance while you're still alive through the use of policy loans. Consequently, not only can insurance policies be used for legacy planning, they are also an invaluable instrument within your retirement planning toolbox.

To understand how this is possible, let's briefly look at how life insurance policies function, in general. There are two main classes of life insurance: **term** and **permanent**. Term life insurance is an idea with which most people are familiar. With term life insurance, you purchase a certain amount of death benefit that will go to your heirs upon your death but this policy will only be in effect for as long as the term of your policy, typically 10 to 20 years. Alternatively, permanent life insurance has no term involved. It will remain in effect throughout your entire life so long as you continue to pay the premiums. This option is often generally accompanied by higher premiums than term insurance for the same amount of death benefit coverage.

As a result of its higher initial cost, many people opt for term insurance and miss out on the benefits of permanent. However, there are significant differences between these two policies that are not often considered during a comparative analysis of the cost between the two policies. For example, it's important to keep in mind how often term life insurance policies actually pay out. Most often, term policies usually expire before the death of the policy-holder.

Very few term policies pay out death benefit claims. Consequently, if your term expires and you still want to have insurance you will have to purchase another policy, which could be an issue for several reasons, not the least of which is that a term policy with the same benefit will be much more expensive than your original policy and, many times, health issues that occurred during the term of your previous policy, such as cancer or a heart condition, may make it impossible to acquire another policy. If this unfortunate event were to occur, your loved ones would be unprotected and you would lose out on all the potential legacy and retirement planning benefits provided by life insurance's tax-advantaged status.

THE PERMANENT BENEFITS OF PERMANENT LIFE INSURANCE

As we learned earlier through the discussion of annuities, insurance companies like predictability so they make long-term investments that will stabilize the amount of money they both pay out and receive. As a result, when you buy a permanent life insurance policy, the life insurance company will invest a certain portion of your premium and then pay interest on this amount. It is the increasing buildup of this interest that accounts for the cash accumulation potential of your policy. Essentially, permanent life insurance policies have, in addition to its death benefit, a cash value or living benefit. The death benefit is the face value of your policy and is how much money your heirs will receive upon your death, whereas the living benefit is how much cash value or interest has accrued within your policy, which can be accessed while you're still alive.

To emphasize the importance of this factor, think of term life insurance like renting a house: you have a home for 10 years that you're putting money into but once the lease is up you won't have any equity and you run the risk of not being able to extend your lease due to any number of reasons. On the other hand, permanent life insurance is similar to owning a home: you know you and your family will always have a roof over your heads and the payments you make build equity within your investment.

In other words, not only does permanent life insurance ensure your family will always be protected regardless of any health changes that may arise but, through the continued payment of your premiums, the value of your policy actually increases. This means that under a permanent policy your policy's value will grow, while a term insurance policy's benefit will remain level. How much your policy's value will grow depends on what kind of policy you purchase. The different ways in which the internal rate of return of a policy is determined is similar to that of an annuity: some policies will have a set rate of return (fixed), others will vary with the market (variable), and still others will offer a guaranteed minimum rate that will increase up to a certain cap if the market does well (indexed).

For example, if you purchased an Index Universal Life Policy (IUL), your policy's rate of return would operate a bit like a fixed index annuity. Basically, when the market would increase, you would keep the gains up to a cap and when the market would decrease, not only would you not lose any money, but you'd actually continue to make a little (probably either one or two percent) because there is a minimum guaranteed rate of return. What's more is that so long as you gave the policy enough time for its cash value to accumulate, you could use policy loans to withdraw money from it regardless of your age. In other words, unlike many other financial vehicles, the money contained within your IUL policy is extremely liquid. For instance, traditional IRAs only allow for very limited account withdrawals without penalties before the age of 59½ years old and taking money out of an annuity before its contract term is over means being charged surrender penalties. That said, you cannot purchase an IUL policy and then immediately draw money out of it. Typically, there is a waiting period in place that must elapse before you can withdraw money so enough time will pass for the cash value of your policy to increase. One final and exceptionally attractive element of an IUL policy is that, unlike other retirement accounts, there are no limits on the amount you can contribute into your IUL policy.

However, permanent life insurance policies are meant to provide you with security and flexibility, not to shelter you from you taxes, which they had the potential to do thanks to their cash accumulation value and tax-free benefits. As such, the government created what's known as a Modified Endowment Contract or MEC. Basically, if a life insurance policy is overfunded it will become an MEC and then any money the policy-holder withdraws from it will be subject to taxation, usually at a level similar to that of income received from an annuity.

So why doesn't everyone have permanent life insurance? For one thing, the premiums associated with permanent life insurance are unavoidably higher than term life insurance because of the flexibility and cash accumulation value it affords to policy-holders. And as mentioned earlier, an additional part of the problem has to do with peoples' misconceptions. Permanent life insurance is generally misconceived as something that is very expensive for a wealth accumulation vehicle because there are mortality charges (fees for the death benefit) that detract from the available returns. Furthermore, those returns do not yield as much as the stock market over the long run. This is why many times you will hear the phrase "buy term and invest the rest," where "term" refers to term insurance and "the rest" refers to the difference between a permanent policy's higher premium and a term policy's lower premium for the same coverage. As the previous comparison of term and permanent life insurance illustrates, this is a woefully incomplete picture. However, there are, of course, situations where a term life insurance policy may be the best tool for you to use. It all comes back to what the needs of your particular situation require. For example, a young couple who recently bought a home may opt to purchase a term life insurance policy just to guarantee that the mortgage would be covered if something were to happen to the breadwinner. Be sure to think about what you need your financial products to accomplish and be sure that the policy you select is the one best-suited to fulfill this purpose.

If you purchase a permanent life insurance policy and work with a financial professional to make sure it is properly designed and utilized, you can leverage your policy to produce tax-free retirement income through the use of policy loans and provide your beneficiaries with a tax-free death benefit. In other words, when the cash accumulation value of a permanent life insurance policy is coupled with the fact that any money it pays out will be untaxed, **permanent life insurance, if wielded properly, can be structured to act as a tax-free retirement account.** As the next chapter will outline, the importance of having a tax-free retirement option cannot be understated.

FINDING THE RIGHT FIT

Depending on the needs of your situation, a permanent life insurance policy is an extremely flexible and creative retirement tool. In essence, it can allow you to become your own bank and create your own family pension plan. If your income or retirement plan calls for a significant amount of liquidity, a permanent life insurance policy may be the best financial tool for you to use in order to help you accomplish this. However, a permanent life insurance policy isn't right for everyone; it all depends on the needs of your particular situation.

When it comes to selecting the permanent life insurance policy that is right for you, there is an impressive array of options at your disposable. From whole life insurance to universal life insurance to all the various types contained therein, there are many different components to keep in mind. Consulting a financial professional is the best way to ensure you select the policy best matched to satisfy the needs of your particular situation. The most important thing to remember is that every person will have different objectives when it comes to retirement planning, which means there is no single tool to use that will create a universally "perfect" retirement plan. Instead, look for tools that are right for your plan. What are the unique requirements of your situation? What are your priorities? What does your income plan tell you about your future needs?

The answers to these questions will vary according to your circumstance and personal preferences. In some cases, it will make sense to have a MEC, in others, using life insurance as a retirement income vehicle may not be a strategy worth employing at all. Although there are as many different financial strategies as there are desired retirement outcomes, the process used to select which tool will best satisfy which need is the same. Once you know what the color of your money is and have figured out how much of it needs to be earmarked for preservation, growth, and income, you can then use new investment strategies to ensure you are drawing from the broadest range possible of potential options.

Remember that it's not difficult to fall into the old habit of positioning every investment decision along a sliding scale where

Safety is at one end and Return is at the other. While it's true that investments that offer greater returns are often exposed to more market volatility and risk, using the concept of Liquidity can help offset the extent to which this occurs and will help you avoid falling into limiting and outdated patterns of thinking. What's more, Liquidity will not only make it easier for you to make the mental shift from an earning and saving financial paradigm to an asset leveraging one, but it will also widen the scope of your financial options, which will help you create a flexible and creative retirement plan that is specially tailored to accommodate your situation and preferences.

Although there is no single "right" retirement plan, let's take a moment to briefly go over some of the financial vehicles for retirement mentioned in this book and list the order of priority each tool places on the three dimensions of an investment:

- Fixed Index Annuity: preservation, income, accumulation
- Permanent Life Insurance: income, preservation, accumulation
- Exchange-traded funds and stocks: accumulation, income, preservation

As you can see, there is not an investment strategy that is capable of maximizing all three factors simultaneously. Depending on your unique situation and risk tolerance, you will have to decide which element is most vital to you and your retirement, and then design a plan accordingly. Working with a financial professional is the best way to create a retirement plan that is comprehensive, easy to understand, and purposeful. Additionally, your financial planner will help you design a retirement plan with a strong tax strategy because, as you will see in the following chapter, taxes can make or break your plan.

CHAPTER 6 RECAP //

- New financial strategies consider every investment to be comprised of three main elements: Safety, Return, and Liquidity. Or, when it comes to retirement investment strategies, Safety can be thought of as preservation, Return as accumulation, and Liquidity as income.

- Because no single financial strategy or tool can maximize all three of these components simultaneously, the goal is to find the most beneficial balance between them.

- By utilizing the concept of Liquidity, you will have a broader financial scope through which you can frame your retirement, which will help you develop more innovative and customizable retirement strategies, such as using life insurance as a wealth accumulation tool.

- There are two basic classes of life insurance: term and permanent. Term life insurance policies are only in effect for a specific length of time and have no cash accumulation value. On the other hand, permanent life insurance policies never expire, so long as the premiums continue to be paid and do have cash accumulation value.

- Any money paid out by a life insurance policy is untaxed.

- Through the use of policy loans, permanent life insurance policies can be used to generate tax-free retirement income.

7

THE FATE OF THE FREE WORLD IS TAXES

Unfortunately, taxes are an unavoidable fact of life. For most of us, taxes are an inconvenient and unwelcome burden with which we are well-acquainted. However, this burden will turn into a crushing weight if having a tax strategy is not an integral component of your retirement plan. Why? Because paying taxes once you've retired is an entirely different ballgame than paying taxes when you're still in the working phase of your life. The truth of the matter is that most retirement planning tools are infected with taxes. In order to stay ahead of the game and fund your retirement instead of Uncle Sam's, you need a purposeful and comprehensive tax strategy that will help you save money, protect your assets, and ensure that your legacy remains intact.

How can a tax form do all that? The answer lies in planning. *Tax planning* and *tax reporting* are two very different things. Most people only *report* their taxes. When tax season rolls around, people pull out their 1040s or use TurboTax to enter their income and taxable assets, and ship it off to Uncle Sam at the IRS. If you use a CPA to report your taxes, you are essentially paying them to record history. You have the option of being proactive with your taxes and to plan for your future by making smart, informed decisions about how taxes affect your overall financial plan.

Louis Brandeis provides one of the best examples illustrating how tax planning works. Brandeis was Associate Justice on the Supreme Court of the United States from 1916 to 1939. Born in Louisville, Kentucky, Brandeis was an intelligent man with a touch of country charm. He described tax planning this way:

"I live in Alexandria, Virginia. Near the Court Chambers, there is a toll bridge across the Potomac. When in a rush, I pay the dollar toll and get home early. However, I usually drive outside the downtown section of the city and cross the Potomac on a free bridge.

The bridge was placed outside the downtown Washington, D.C. area to serve a useful social service – getting drivers to drive the extra mile and help alleviate congestion during the rush hour.

If I went over the toll bridge and through the barrier without paying a toll, I would be committing tax evasion.

If I drive the extra mile and drive outside the city of Washington to the free bridge, I am using a legitimate, logical and suitable method of tax avoidance, and I am performing a useful social service by doing so.

*The tragedy is that **few people know that the free bridge exists.**"*

Like Brandeis, most American taxpayers have options when it comes to "crossing the Potomac," so to speak. It's a financial planner's job to tell you what options are available. Think of it this way: you can wait until March to file, at which time you might pay someone to report your taxes for you and you could very well end up paying the government a larger portion of your income than necessary.

Or, you can instead file before the end of the year and work with your financial professional to incorporate a tax plan as part of your overall financial planning strategy. Filing later is like crossing the toll bridge. Tax planning is like crossing the free bridge. Which would you rather do?

The answer to this question is easy. Most people want to save money and pay less in taxes. What makes this situation really difficult in real life, however, is that the signs along the side of the road that direct us to the free bridge are not that clear. To normal Americans, and to plenty of people who have studied it, the U.S. tax code is easy to get lost in. There are all kinds of rules, exceptions to rules, caveats and conditions that are difficult to understand, or even to know of their existence. What you really need to know is your options and the impact those options will have on your bottom line.

Working with a financial professional who, along with a CPA, makes recommendations about your finances to you, will keep you looking forward instead of in the rearview mirror as you enter retirement.

A TAXING JOB

When you retire, you move from the earning and accumulation phase of your life into the asset distribution phase of your life. As you learned in the chapter on Social Security, once you enter the distribution phase of your life *saving* money basically becomes more profitable than *making* it, which means you want to take as little money as possible from your nest egg and instead leverage your assets so they will be able to generate income for you.

To put it another way, wherever you have put your Green Money for retirement, you are going to start relying on it to provide you with the income that once came as a paycheck. For most people, this means relying on Social Security, a 401(k), an IRA, or a pension. Most of these distributions will be considered income by the IRS and will be taxed as such. There are exceptions to that (not all of your Social Security income is taxed, and income from Roth IRAs is not taxed), but for the most part, your distributions will be subject to income taxes.

Regarding assets that you have in an IRA or a 401(k) plan that uses an IRA, when you reach 70 ½ years of age, you will be required to draw a certain amount of money from your IRA as income each year. That amount is called a Required Minimum Distribution (RMD) and is determined by your age and the balance in your IRA. Why are you required to withdraw money from your own account? Chances are the money in that account has grown over time, and the government wants to collect taxes on that growth. If you have a large balance in an IRA, there's a chance your RMD could increase your income significantly enough to put you into a higher tax bracket, subjecting you to a higher tax rate. At this stage in your life, what really impacts you is how much of the money produced by your income-generating assets you are able to keep in your pocket after taxes.

However, the unfortunate fact of the matter is that the money you most need to protect and preserve is contained within accounts that are infected with taxes. You need to understand the tax implications of your retirement strategy before you enter the distribution phase of your plan because **you will make more money saving on taxes than you will by making more money**. If you can reduce your tax burden by 30, 20 or even 10 percent, you earn yourself that much more money by not paying it in taxes.

How do you save money on taxes? By having a plan. In this instance, a financial professional can work with the CPAs at their firm to create a **distribution plan** that minimizes your taxes and maximizes your annual net income.

NOT ALL MONEY IS CREATED EQUALLY

In order to develop and implement an effective tax strategy, it is first important to understand what types of money exist and how each of these will be taxed during both the accumulation process and the distribution process. Given the vastly different levels of taxation each type is subjected to, it becomes apparent that, when it comes to taxes, not all money is created equally. Basically, there are four types of money:

1. Free money
2. Tax-advantaged money
3. Tax-deferred money
4. Taxable money
   a. Ordinary income
   b. Capital gains and qualified dividends

FREE MONEY

Free money is exactly what it sounds like: money that is yours but that you didn't have to earn. It's the best kind of money regardless of tax treatment because, in the end, you still end up with more money than you would have otherwise. Many employers will provide contributions toward employee retirement accounts to offer additional employment benefits and encourage employees to save for their own retirement. With this, employers often will offer a matching contribution in which they contribute up to a certain percentage of an employee's salary (generally three to five percent) toward that employee's retirement account when the employee contributes to their retirement account as well. For example, if an employee earns $50,000 annually and contributes three percent ($1,500) to their retirement account annually, the employer will also contribute three percent ($1,500) to the employee's account. That is $1,500 in free money. Take all you can get! Bear in mind that any employer contribution to a 401(k) will still be subject to taxation when withdrawn.

TAX-ADVANTAGED MONEY: MUNICIPAL BONDS

Tax-advantaged money is the next best thing to free money. Although you have to earn tax-advantaged money, you do not have to give part of it away to Uncle Sam. Tax-advantaged money technically comes in four basic forms that you can utilize during your lifetime. However, the fourth option is only available to you if you're in prison, so for our intents and purposes there are really only three types of tax-advantaged money worth discussing.

One of the most commonly known forms of tax-advantaged money is municipal bonds, which earn and pay interest that could be tax-advantaged on the federal level, or state level, or both. There are several caveats that should be discussed with regard to the notion of tax-advantaged income from municipal bonds. First, you will notice that tax-advantaged has several flavors from the state and federal perspective. This is because states will generally tax the interest earned on a municipal bond unless the bond is offered from an entity located within that state. This severely limits the availability of completely tax-advantaged municipal bonds and constrains underlying risk and liquidity factors. Second, municipal bond interest is added back into the equation for determining your modified adjusted gross income (MAGI) for Social Security. This could push your income above a threshold and subject a portion of your Social Security income to taxation. In effect, if this interest subjects some other income to taxation then this interest is truly being taxed.

Last, municipal bond interest may be excluded from the regular federal tax system, but it is included for determining tax under the alternative minimum tax (AMT) system. In its basic form, the AMT system is a separate tax system that applies if the tax computed under AMT exceeds the tax computed under the regular tax system. The difference between these two computations is the alternative minimum tax.

TAX-ADVANTAGED MONEY: ROTH IRA AND ROTH 401(K)

Roth accounts are probably the single greatest tax asset that has come from Congress outside of life insurance. They are well known but rarely used. Roth IRAs were first established by the Taxpayer Relief Act of 1997 and named after Senator William Roth, the chief sponsor of the legislation. Roth accounts are simply an account in the form of an individual retirement account or an employer sponsored retirement account that allows for tax-advantaged growth of earnings and, thus, tax-advantaged income.

The main difference between a Roth and a traditional IRA or employer-sponsored plan lies in the timing of the taxation. We are all very familiar with the typical scenario of putting money away for retirement through an employer plan, whereby they deduct money from our paychecks and put it directly into a retirement account. This money is taken out before taxes are calculated, meaning we do not pay tax on those earnings today. A Roth account, on the other hand, takes the money after the taxes have been removed and puts it into the retirement account, so we do pay tax on the money today. The other significant difference between these two is taxation during distribution in later years. Regarding our traditional retirement accounts, when we take the money out later it is added to our ordinary income and is taxed accordingly. Additionally, including this in our income subjects us to the consequences mentioned above for municipal bonds with Social Security taxation, AMT, as well as higher Medicare premiums. A Roth on the other hand is distributed tax-advantaged and does not contribute toward negative impact items such as Social Security taxation, AMT, or Medicare premium increases. It essentially comes back to us without tax and other obligations.

The best way to view the difference between the two accounts is to look at the life of a farmer. A farmer will buy seed, plant it in the ground, grow the crops and harvest it later for sale. Typically, the farmer would only pay tax on the crops that have been harvested and sold. But if you were the farmer, would you rather pay tax on the $5,000 of seed that you plant today or the $50,000 of crops harvested later? The obvious answer is $5,000 of seed today. The truth to the matter is that you are a farmer, except you plant dollars into your retirement account instead of seeds into the earth.

So why doesn't everyone have a Roth retirement account if things are so simple? There are several reasons, but the single greatest reason has been the constraints on contributions. If you earned over certain thresholds (MAGI over $125,000 single and $183,000 joint for 2012), you were not eligible to make contributions, and until last year, if your modified adjusted gross income (MAGI) was over $100,000 (single or joint), you could not convert a traditional IRA to a Roth. In addition to the obstacle posed by these contribution limits, Roth accounts are not particularly well understood because most people have been educated to believe that saving on taxes today is the best possible course of action. Consequently, few employers offer Roth options in their retirement plans and, as most people save for retirement through their employers, this has prevented the use of Roth IRAs from becoming widespread.

Likewise, a Roth 401(k) plan works much in the same way as a Roth IRA: you would pay taxes on the money before you contributed it to your 401(k), so that the money distributed by the account would be tax-free. Although if your employer matched your contributions to this account, their contributions would be put into a pre-tax account and would later be subject to taxation during distribution. One of the additional benefits of a Roth 401(k) is that it does not have any income limitations. However, like Roth IRAs, Roth 401(k) plans have also been slow to take root because of people's lack of knowledge about them.

TAX-ADVANTAGED MONEY: LIFE INSURANCE

As you learned in the previous chapter, money paid out by a life insurance policy is not taxed, which makes life insurance the most significant tax asset to have ever been created by Congress. Life insurance is the little-known or little-discussed tax asset that holds some of the greatest value in your financial history both during life and upon death. Regardless of what type of life insurance policy you purchase, no one has to pay taxes on any money received from it, which makes it the best tax-advantaged device available by far. For example, if your life insurance policy is used only as a legacy-planning tool, the death benefit your heirs receive will not be taxed, nor will it affect the taxation of their other assets in any way. Likewise, if you purchased a permanent life insurance policy so its cash accumulation potential could be harnessed to allow it to function as a retirement planning tool, any income generated by the policy would also be tax-free.

The utility of life insurance's tax-free nature cannot be understated: of the four phases of retirement planning (contribution, accumulation, distribution, and transfer), only the contribution stage is subjected to taxation, which allows the funds within a permanent life insurance policy to grow tax-free, be withdrawn tax-free, and be transferred to beneficiaries tax-free. Thus, even though life insurance is typically only thought of as having a "death benefit," it can also be designed to function as a living benefit if it is structured properly. Put more simply, a permanent life insurance policy can act as a tax-free retirement account if it is correctly formulated.

TAX-DEFERRED MONEY

Most people are familiar with the idea of tax-deferred money. Essentially, tax-deferred money is money that is put into an investment vehicle and allowed to accumulate tax-free. The earnings grown in these accounts are only taxed once they are distributed, at which point, they will be treated as income and taxed accordingly. The most frequently encountered types of tax-deferral vehicles are the traditional IRA or a non-qualified annuity. While it is quite common to come across tax-deferred money, its appeal can sometimes be misleading. On the one hand, being able to defer paying taxes allows for tax-deferred growth, while on the other, too much growth that is not properly planned for can result in a tax time-bomb that is just waiting to go off in your account.

TAXABLE MONEY
Taxable money is everything else and is taxable today, later or whenever it is received.

TO QUALIFY OR NOT TO QUALIFY
In addition to the tax implications for the above four types of money, investment money also has its own unique set of taxation. For tax purposes, there are basically two kinds of investment money: qualified and non-qualified. While there are many differences between qualified and non-qualified investments, the main difference is this: the money invested in a qualified plan is tax deferred until it is withdrawn whereas non-qualified investments require you to pay taxes on the money you put into them and, depending on the type of non-qualified investment you use, you may also have to pay taxes on its returns.

Ideally, the benefit of having a qualified investment would be that you could put money into it throughout your career so that it could grow freely without being subjected to the higher tax rates that your working income would put you in. Once you retire, your lack of working income would put you into a lower tax bracket, so when you withdraw money from the investment and finally paid taxes on it, the money would be taxed at a lower rate than it otherwise would have been. However, this entire perspective is contingent upon the idea that tax rates will still be at current levels.

As you will learn about in more depth later in this chapter, tax rates are at a historic low and are only going to go in one direction: up. Consequently, while qualified investment tools may help you realize more growth initially, you will have to pay taxes on those returns eventually. When you finally do, taxes will be higher, which would mean a qualified investment cost you more money in the long run. To put it more plainly, qualified investments are infected with taxes. It makes more sense to pay taxes today while the rates are lower, because this will ultimately help you to save money. By making a plan and paying taxes today, you will save money for tomorrow.

However, bear in mind that the key here is balance: there are times when qualified investments may be a useful component within your overall financial strategy. Again, it all depends on the needs of your situation and the tax strategy you and your financial professional develop to help you maximize your net income. One scenario in which a qualified investment might be a good choice is if you have a portion of your investment portfolio that is being actively traded. In this case, there would be a high amount of buying and selling of stocks, bonds, etc., and most every transaction would be a taxable event if they were kept in a non-qualified account. If the goal of those assets was to just stay in the market, not only would all that taxation cut into their returns and make it harder for them to grow, but it would also be frustrating to constantly pay taxes on assets for which you had no immediate plan of distribution. However, if you put them inside a qualified account, such as an IRA, you would be able to realize the higher gains of those investments without paying tax on their growth every year. Even in this scenario, however, a qualified investment could be a very risky choice: if an IRA experiences a lot of growth, the amount of taxes that will need to be paid grows right along with it, which could create big problems for your retirement plan down the road.

Ultimately, different investment strategies will have different effects on how your investments will be taxed. If you are interested in taking advantage of tax strategies that maximize your net income, you need the attentive strategies, experience and knowledge of a professional who can give you options that position you for profit. At the end of the day, what's important to you as the consumer is how much you keep, your after-tax take home.

MAKING TAXES WORK FOR YOU

The greatest difference when comparing taxable and tax-advantaged income is a function of how much money we keep after tax. For help in determining what the differences should be, excluding outside factors such as Social Security taxation and AMT, a tax equivalent yield should be used.

To put the tax equivalent yield into perspective, let us look at an example: Steve and Laticia are retired, living on their Social Security benefits and the interest from their investments. Currently, they are falling within the 25 percent tax bracket. They have a substantial portion of their investments in municipal bonds yielding 6 percent, which is quite comforting in today's market. The tax equivalent yield they would need to earn from a taxable investment would be 8 percent, a 2 percent gap that seems almost impossible given current market volatility. However, something that has never been put into perspective is that the interest from their municipal bonds is subject to taxation on their Social Security benefits (at 21.25 percent). With this, the yield on their municipal bonds would be 4.725 percent, and the taxable equivalent yield falls to 6.3 percent, leaving a gap of only 1.575 percent.

In the end, most people spend their lives accumulating wealth through the best, if not the only vehicle they know, a tax-deferred account. This account is most likely a 401(k) or 403(b) plan offered through their employer and may be supplemented with an IRA that was established at one point or another. However, most people are unaware that these accounts are riddled with taxes and as the years go by, they blindly throw money into these accounts in an effort to save for a retirement they someday hope to reach.

The truth is, most people have an age selected for when they would like to retire, but spend their lives wondering if they will ever be able to actually quit working. To answer this question, you must understand how much money you will have available to contribute toward your needs. *In other words, you need to know what your after-tax income will be during this period.*

Ultimately, if you don't take the time today to develop a tax strategy that can work in conjunction with your retirement plan, you may be exposing yourself to excessive taxation and putting your retirement at risk.

TAXATION NATION

The importance of developing a tax strategy becomes even more apparent when you consider the fact that tax legislation over the course of American history has left one very resounding message: taxes go up. However, tax hikes usually do not go into effect until two or three years after their introduction and even then they often take place through a series of smaller increases instead of happening all at once. Consequently, the idea of rising taxes has become such a familiar menace that it has begun to sound like an empty threat. This is quite far from the truth: despite its piecemeal implementation, taxes are increasing. The result of this prolonged implementation period can be equated to death by a thousand paper cuts.

RAISE THE ROOF: THE CAUSE AND EFFECTS OF THE DEBT CEILING

The raising of the debt ceiling raised more than just the ability for our government to go further into debt. It also raised concerns and fears about the future of our economy. We are now seeing major swings in the markets with investors showing serious concerns over the future of investment valuations and their personal wealth. Unfortunately, the reasoning behind all of this uncertainty is preceded by the inability to see the full implications of what is in store. We rarely talk about the fact that the discussions on raising the debt ceiling were coupled to discussions on major tax reforms needed to correct the problems underlining the debt ceiling increase itself.

Increasing the debt ceiling was needed because the government maxed out its credit card, so to speak, which it has been living off of for quite some time. It is really not much different than what we have been seeing from the general public for the past few decades. Unfortunately, most of us do not have the ability to get a credit limit increase on our credit cards once we reach the maximum limit unless we can show the ability to pay this balance back. The only way to pay this credit card back is by spending less and making more money.

This is exactly where the federal government is today. They have been given a higher credit limit, but they still must find a way to decrease the spending while making more money. The only way the government makes money is by collecting taxes. Unfortunately, at the current moment, the government is collecting approximately $120 billion less per month than it currently spends. Discussions for major tax reform have accompanied the discussions for the increased debt ceiling.

DEBT AND EARNINGS

Let us take a closer look at where we are today. The U.S. national debt is increasing at an alarming rate, rising to levels never seen before and threatening serious harm to the economy. Through the end of 2010, the national debt has risen to $13.6 trillion, averaging an 11.4 percent increase annually over the past five years and a 9.2 percent increase annually over the past 10 years. To put this into perspective, the national gross domestic product (GDP) has increased to $14.5 trillion during the same period, averaging a 2.9 percent annual increase over the past five years and a 3.9 percent increase over the past 10 years. At the end of 2010, the national debt level was 93 percent of the GDP. Economists believe that a sustainable economy exists at a maximum level of approximately 80 percent. As of December 20, 2013, the U.S. national debt is 107.69 percent of GDP with the debt at $17.252 trillion and the GDP at $16.020 trillion.*

The significance of these two numbers lies within the contrast. The national debt is the amount that needs to be repaid. This is the credit card balance. Gross domestic product on the other hand is less known and represents the market value of all final goods and services produced within a country during a given period. Essentially, GDP represents the gross taxable income available to the government. If debts are increasing at a greater rate than the gross income available for taxation, then the only way to make up the difference is by increasing the rate at which the gross income is taxed.

The most recent presidential budget shows a continuing trend in the disparity between growth in the national debt and GDP over the next two decades. Although the increasing disparity is a real concern and shows that, at least in the short run, the federal deficit will not be addressed to counteract the potential crisis ahead, it is the revenue collection that tells the disconcerting story. Over the past 40 years the average collection of GDP has been approximately 17.6 percent and currently collections are at approximately 14.4 percent of GDP.

As the presidential budget reveals, the projected revenues are estimated to be 20 percent by the end of the next decade. That is a 38.8 percent increase from the current tax levels. To put this into

---

*http://www.usdebtclock.org/ 12/20/13

perspective, if you are currently in the top tax bracket of 35 percent and this bracket increases by the proposed collection increase, your tax rate will be approximately 48.5 percent. Keep in mind that even at this rate the deficit is projected to increase.

2013 – THE END OF AN ERA?

From a historical point of view, taxes are extremely low. The last time the U.S. national debt was at the same percentage level of GDP as today was at the end of World War II and several years following. The maximum tax rate averaged 90 percent from 1944 through 1963. Compare that to the maximum rate of 35 percent today and it becomes very clear that there is a disparity of extreme proportion.

Taxes during this historical period were at extreme levels for nearly 20 years, during and following this current level of debt-to-GDP. A significant point to note about the difference between that time and today is the economic activity. The period of 1944 through 1963 was in the heart of both the industrial revolution and the birth of the Baby Boom generation. Today, we are mired in extreme volatility with frequent periods of boom and bust at the same time we are witnessing the beginning of the greatest retirement wave ever experienced within the U.S. economy.

To contrast these two time periods in respect to the recovery period is senseless as the external pressures from globalization and domestic unfunded liabilities did not exist or were irrelevant factors during the prior period.

To add insult to injury, U.S. domestic unfunded liabilities are currently estimated somewhere around $61.6 trillion above due to items such as Social Security, Medicare and government pensions. The most concerning part of this pertains to the coming wave of retirement as the Baby Boom generation begins retiring and drawing on the unfunded Social Security for which they currently have entitlement. Over the long run, expenditures related to healthcare programs such as Medicare and Medicaid are projected to grow faster than the economy overall as the population matures.

To put unfunded liabilities into perspective, consider these as off-balance-sheet obligations similar to those of Enron. Although these are not listed as part of the national debt, they must be paid. These liabilities exist outside of the annual budgetary debt discussed. The difference between Enron and the U.S. unfunded liabilities is that if the U.S. government cannot come up with the funds to pay all these liabilities through revenue generation, they will print the money necessary to pay the debt.

WHERE DO WE GO FROM HERE?

Unfortunately, the general public is in a no-win situation for this solution to the problem. Printing money does not bode well for economic growth. This creates inflationary pressures that devalue the U.S. dollar and make everyone less wealthy. Cutting the entitlements that compose this liability leaves millions of people without benefits they have come to expect. The only other option, and one that the government knows all too well, is increasing taxes. In fact, according to a Congressional Budget Office paper issued in 2004:

"The term 'unfunded liability' has been used to refer to a gap between the government's projected financial commitment under a particular program and the revenues that are expected to be available to fund that commitment. But no government obligation can be truly considered 'unfunded' because of the U.S. government's sovereign power to tax – which is the ultimate resource to meet its obligations."

A balanced budget will be required at some point and with this will come higher taxes. We have uncertainty surrounding tax rates and how high they will go. At that time, extensions put in place in December 2010 on Bush-era tax cuts are set to expire. We are likely to see some tax increases at this point. Whether it is only on the top earners or unilaterally across all income levels is yet to be seen, but an increase of some sort will most certainly occur.

How do you prepare? Why spend so much time reassuring you that taxes will increase? Because you have an opportunity to take action. Now is the time to prepare for what will come and structure countermeasures for the good, the bad and the ugly of each of these legislative nightmares through tax-advantaged retirement planning.

You make more money by saving on taxes than you do by making more money. The simplistic logic of the statement makes sense when you discover it takes $1.50 in earnings to put that same dollar, saved in taxes, back in your pocket.

As simple as it sounds, it is much more difficult to execute. Most people fail to put together a plan as they near retirement, beginning with a simple cash flow budget. If you have not analyzed your proposed income streams and expenses, you could not possibly have taken the time to position these cash flows and other events into a tax-preferred plan.

Most people will state that they have a plan and, thus, do not need any further assistance in this area. The truth in most instances is that people could not show you their plan, and among the few that could, most would not be able to show you how they have executed it. In this regard, they might as well be Richard Nixon stating, "I am not a crook" for as much as they state, "I have a plan." The truth lies in waiting. As we approach or begin retirement, we should look at what cash flows we will have. Do we have a pension? How about Social Security? How much additional cash flow am I going to need to draw from my assets to maintain the lifestyle that I desire?

We spend our whole lives saving and accumulating wealth but spend so little time determining how to distribute this accumulation so as to retain it. We need to make sure we have the appropriate diversification of taxable versus non-taxable assets to complement our distribution strategy. Ultimately, it's more important than ever to save money on taxes.

All else being equal, it would not matter if you put your money into a taxable, tax-deferred or tax-advantaged account as long as income tax rates never change and outside factors are never an event. The net amount you receive in the end will be the same. Unfortunately, this will never be the case. We already know that taxes will increase in the future, meaning we will likely see higher taxes in retirement than during our peak earning years.

Regardless, saving for retirement in any form is a good thing as it appears from all practical perspectives that future government benefits will be cut and taxes will increase. You have the ability to plan today for efficient tax diversification and maximization of your after-tax dollars during your distribution years.

CHAPTER 7 RECAP //

- Once you retire, you will make more money by saving on taxes than you will by actually making more money. Having a tax strategy in place will help you to minimize your taxes and maximize your income.
- Reporting your taxes is basically just an expensive way to document your financial history. When you work with a financial professional to develop a *plan* for your taxes you are creating a roadmap for your future.
- There are four kinds of money: free money, tax-advantaged money, tax-deferred money, and taxable money.
- Permanent life insurance policies can be designed to function as a tax-free retirement account.
- Qualified investments are infected with taxes, which is why you need to have a strategy to mitigate their impact on your retirement plan.
- In all likelihood, as the national debt continues to rise, so will our taxes. Consider utilizing retirement strategies that have you paying taxes now, so you can take advantage of today's lower rates, instead of having to pay them in the future, when the rates will probably be higher.

8

COVERING YOUR (TAX) BASES

So far, so good: avoid taxes, maximize your net annual income and have a plan for doing it. When people decide to leverage the experience and resources of a financial professional, they may not be thinking of how distribution planning and tax planning will benefit their portfolios. Often more exciting prospects like planning income annuities, investing in the market and structuring investments for growth rule the day. As you know, taxes play a crucial role in retirement planning. Achieving your tax goals requires knowledge of options, foresight and professional guidance.

Finding the path to a good tax plan isn't always a simple task. Every tax return you file is different from the one before it because things constantly change. Your expenses change. Planned or unplanned purchases occur. Health care costs, medical bills, an inheritance, property purchases, reaching an age where your RMD kicks in or travel, any number of things can affect how much income you report and how many deductions you take each year.

Preparing for the ever-changing landscape of your financial life requires a tax-diversified portfolio that includes a healthy balance of each of the four types of money outlined in the previous chapter so you will be better positioned to leverage the incomes, expenditures and deductions that affect you each year.

A financial professional will work with you to answer questions like these:

- What does your tax landscape look like?
- Do you have a tax-diversified portfolio robust enough to adapt to your needs?
- Do you have a diversity of taxable and non-taxable income planned for your retirement?
- Will you be able to maximize your distributions to take advantage of your deductions when you retire?
- Is your portfolio strong enough and tax-diversified enough to adapt to an ever-changing (and usually increasing) tax code?

» *Just after Pat celebrated her 78th birthday, she had to have a hip replacement. Not a great way to start a new year! But the surgery went smoothly and Pat was soon able to return home and call her son, brother, and best friend to let them know how her recovery is progressing. Pat should have added her CPA to her list of people to call. Pat's medical expenses for the procedure, her hospital stay, her medications, and her ongoing physical therapy ended up costing more than $50,000.*

Currently, Americans can deduct medical expenses that are more than 7.5 percent of their Adjusted Gross Income (AGI). The year of Pat's hip replacement, her AGI was $60,000, which means she can deduct $44,000 of her medical bills from her taxes that year. According to her AGI, Pat is eligible to deduct more than 80 percent of her medical expenses that year, but **Pat didn't know this***.*

Had she been working with a financial professional who regularly asked her about any changes in her life, her spending, or her expenses (expected or unexpected), Pat could have saved thousands of dollars. Pat can also file an amendment to her tax return to recoup the overpayment.

This relatively simple example of how tax planning can save you money is just the tip of the iceberg. No one can be expected to know the entire U.S. tax code. But a professional who is working with a team of CPAs and financial professionals have an advantage over the average taxpayer who must start from square one on their own every year. Have you been taking advantage of all the deductions that are available to you?

PROACTIVE TAX PLANNING

The implications of proactive tax planning are far reaching, and are larger than many people realize. Remember, doing your taxes in January, February, March or April means you are writing a history book. Planning your taxes in October, November or December means that you are writing the story as it happens. You can look at all the factors that are at play and make decisions that will impact your tax return *before* you file it.

Realizing that tax planning is an aspect of financial planning is an important leap to make. **When you incorporate tax planning into your financial planning strategy, it becomes part of the way you maximize your financial potential** because paying less in taxes means you keep more of your money. Simply put, the more money you keep, the more of it you can leverage as an asset. This kind of planning can affect you at any stage of your life. If you are 40 years old, are you contributing the maximum amount to your 401(k) plan? Are you contributing to a Roth IRA? Are you finding ways to structure the savings you are dedicating to your children's education? Do you have life insurance? Taxes and tax planning affects all of these investment tools. Having a relationship with a professional who works with a CPA can help you build a truly comprehensive financial plan that not only works with your investments, but also shapes your assets to find the most efficient ways to prepare for tax time. There may be years that you could benefit from higher distributions because of the tax bracket that you are in, or there could be years you would benefit from taking less. There may be years when you have a lot of deductions and years you have relatively few. **Adapting your distributions to work in concert with your available deductions** is at the heart of smart tax planning. Professional guidance can bring you to the next level of income distribution, allowing you to remain flexible enough to maximize your tax efficiency. And remember, saving money on taxes makes you more money than making money does.

What you have on paper is important: your assets, savings, investments, which are financial expression of your work and time. It's just as important to know how to get it off the paper in a way that keeps most of it in your pocket. Almost anything that involves financial planning also involves taxes. Annuities, investments, IRAs, 401(k)s, 403(b)s, and many other investment options will have tax implications. Life also has a way of throwing curveballs. Illness, expensive car repair or replacement, or *any event that has a financial impact on your life will likely have a corresponding tax implication* around which you should adapt your financial plan. Tax planning helps you do just that.

Developing a tax strategy is important at every stage of your life. From accumulating your wealth during your working years to distributing it during your retirement, to transferring it to your heirs as part of your legacy, taxes can be the difference between successfully satisfying your needs or not. **Without proper planning, one dollar can end up being less than 25 cents to your heirs.**

» *Terry's father, George, recently passed away at the age of 82. When George was a boy, he had to choose between finishing school and getting a job to support his family. He chose immediate employment over education and although he never regretted the decision, he wanted to make sure his heirs would never come face-to-face with a similar choice so he made his son Terry the beneficiary of his $500,000 IRA. Terry has a wife and four children, two of whom are just about to enter college. Terry knows his father wanted most of the IRA to go toward funding his children's college educations so after George's estate is distributed, Terry liquidates the IRA. Little did Terry know that this one seemingly small decision will trigger a massively taxable event: because of the IRA, Terry's taxable income for that year now puts him in a 39.6 percent tax bracket, immediately reducing the value of the asset to $302,000. An additional 3.8 percent surtax on net investment income further diminishes the funds to $283,000. Liquidating the IRA in effect subjects much of Terry's regular income to the surtax, as well. At this point, Terry will be taxed at 43.4 percent.*

Terry's state taxes are an additional 9 percent. Moreover, estate taxes on George's assets claim another 22 percent. By the time the IRS is through, Terry's income from the IRA will be taxed at 75 percent, leaving him with $125,000 of the original $500,000. While it would help contribute to the education of his children, it wouldn't come anywhere near completely paying for it, something the $500,000 could have easily done.

As the above example makes clear, leaving an asset to your beneficiaries can be more complicated than it may seem. In the case of a traditional IRA, after federal, estate and state taxes, the asset could literally diminish to as little as 25 percent of its value. The government doesn't just tax your income from investments while you're alive: they will also dip into your legacy so it's vital to plan accordingly. Although estate taxes aren't as hot of a topic as they were a few years ago, they are still an issue of concern for many people with assets. While taxes may not apply on estates that are less than $5 million, certain states have estate taxes with much lower exclusion ratios. Some are as low as $600,000. Many people may have to pay a state estate tax. One strategy for avoiding those types of taxes is to move assets outside of your estate. That can include gifting them to family or friends, putting them into an irrevocable trust or purchasing a life insurance policy.

A financial professional can help you make smarter tax decisions with your own finances because any professional worth their salt will be working with a firm that has a team of trained tax professionals, including CPAs, who will have an intimate knowledge of the tax code and how to adapt a financial plan to it.

Here's another example of how taxes have major implications on asset management:

> *» Cynthia and Frank are a 64-year-old couple and have been married for 22 years. Recently, they began working with a financial professional, Alice, to help them get a better handle on their finances and retirement planning. They've made many positive changes and are feeling confident and excited to enter into their Golden Years together. For example, they've restructured their assets so they fall within their risk tolerance comfort zone and created assets that will provide them with Green Money income once they retire. In addition, they figured out when and how to file for Social Security to maximize their benefit, discovered they have several options to help them fill their income gap, and have worked with Alice to design a Yellow Money strategy to help them invest the money that is left over. After most everything is squared away, Alice asks them about their tax plan and Cynthia and Frank tell her they're very happy with how their CPA handles their taxes every year.*

Alice explains she's not interested in who helps them do their taxes, she's interested in who helps them do their tax planning. Cynthia and Frank realize they don't have a good answer to that question.

They decide to bring their financial plan to the CPA who works at the same firm as Alice and have her run a tax projection for them. A couple days later, Alice calls them with a tax plan for the next year that would save them more than $5,000 on their tax return. Cynthia and Frank are shocked and elated. A simple piece of advice from the CPA based on the numbers revealed that if they paid their estimated taxes before the end of the year, they would be able to itemize it as a deduction, allowing them to save thousands of dollars.

This solution won't work for everyone, and it may not work for Cynthia and Frank every year. But that's not the point: what matters here is that by being proactive with their approach to taxes and using the resources made available by their financial professional, they were able to create a tax plan that saved them money.

TAKING CONTROL OF YOUR PLAN

At this point, you're probably on board with the fact that the less you pay in taxes, the better. After all, this is your money for your retirement and you want to keep it that way. In order to have the retirement you want, you need to develop a plan that includes as much tax-free income as possible. Luckily, there are a variety of strategies you can use to accomplish this.

The first thing to consider is that your 401(k) is so plagued with taxes that it is a tool for Uncle Sam's retirement, not yours: it is a government plan that plays by its own rules. For example, one such rule is that if you take money out of your 401(k) before you are 59 ½ years old, a 10 percent withdrawal penalty may apply. To take control of your 401(k) and make it work for you instead of the other way around, you can transfer the plan into an IRA so you will have more control over your retirement investment options. The easiest way to do this is by working with a financial professional who can help you perform a trustee-to-trustee transfer. If you incorrectly attempt to transfer your 401(k) into an IRA, you will be subject to further taxation and fees.

> » *Ellen just celebrated her 49th birthday and has begun thinking about what the next half of her life will bring. For the first time, retirement no longer seems like a fanciful notion, but something that's just over the horizon. With this realization, Ellen is suddenly much more aware of the fact that all her retirement money is wrapped up in a 401(k) she knows next to nothing about. Ellen decides to take control of her future and transfer at least some of her money from a 401(k) to an IRA. She's heard people talk about doing an "IRA rollover" before and, after a quick bit of research, it doesn't sound too hard to do. It seems like all she needs to do is decide how much money she wants to rollover, request the money from her employer, and then deposit it into her new IRA. The following day, Ellen bumps into an old friend, Dana, outside her favorite coffee shop.*
>
> *As it just so happens, Dana works in finance so Ellen decides to ask her for any last minute advice before she does the rollover and it's a good thing she does! Dana explains to Ellen that the moment she requests a check for the $50,000 she was going to take out of her 401(k) to put into her new IRA, she would have triggered a taxable event. This would mean that, due to regulatory requirements, her employer would have to withhold 20 percent ($10,000) of that money for federal taxes and would only be able to write her a check for $40,000, meaning that Ellen would have to pay for the rest out of pocket. That's a lot of money to just have on hand! If Ellen wasn't able to cover*

that difference and decided to settle for only depositing $40,000 into her IRA, the elusive $10,000 that wasn't rolled over into her IRA would be treated as ordinary income and could be hit with an early-distribution penalty. Ellen is shocked: she had no idea that something that seemed so simple could end up being so costly. Dana explains that the best thing for her to do is a trustee-to-trustee transfer, which would rollover her assets directly from her employer to the bank holding her IRA. This would keep Ellen's money safe from all those taxes and fees. They make plans to meet later in the week so Dana can help Ellen do just that!

This is not to say that all 401(k)s are all bad all the time: they can be incredibly useful up to a point. For example, when your employer contributes to your account they are giving you free retirement money. At that point, funding your account up to the match will let you use your 401(k) as a savings vehicle, just be sure to mind the numbers. If, for instance, your employer matches up to four percent and you've been putting 10 percent into your account, a better strategy might be to put four percent into your 401(k) and put the remaining six percent into a life insurance policy.

However, if your employer is not matching the funds you put into your 401(k) or if you're simply ready for a retirement plan that gives you more options and control, with fewer taxes, it may be time to consider a Roth IRA.

A Roth IRA is one way to create a tax-free income stream and avoid some of the potentially damaging tax implications, such as Required Minimum Distributions (RMD), inherent within traditional IRAs. With a traditional IRA, when you turn 70 ½ years old you are required to take a minimum amount of money out of your account. This is your RMD and it is treated as taxable income. Roth IRAs, however, do not have RMDs, and their distributions are not taxable. This fact alone makes it very much within your best interest to explore the possibility of moving some of your assets into a Roth account.

ROTH YOUR WHILE

While having a Roth IRA as part of your portfolio is a good idea, converting assets to a Roth IRA can pose some challenges, depending on what kinds of assets you want to transfer.

One common option is the conversion of a traditional IRA to a Roth IRA. You may have heard about converting your IRA to a Roth IRA, but you might not know the full net result on your income. The main difference between the two accounts is that the growth of investments within a traditional IRA is not taxed until income is withdrawn from the account, whereas taxes are charged on contribution amounts to a Roth IRA, not withdrawals. The problem, however, is that when assets are removed from a traditional IRA, even if the assets are being transferred to a Roth IRA account, taxes apply.

There are a lot of reasons to look at Roth conversions. People have a lot of money in IRAs, up to multiple millions of dollars. Even with $500,000, when they turn 70.5 years old, their RMD is going to be approximately $18,000, and they have to take that out whether they want to or not. It's a tax issue. Essentially, if you will be subject to high RMDs, it could impact how much of your Social Security is taxable, and on your tax bracket.

By paying taxes now instead of later on assets in a Roth IRA, you can realize tax-advantaged growth. You pay once and you're done paying. Your heirs are done paying. It's a powerful tool. Here's a simple example to show you how powerful it can be:

Imagine that you pay to convert a traditional IRA to a Roth IRA. You have decided that you want to put the money in a vehicle that gives you a tax-advantaged income option down the road. If you pay a 25 percent tax on that conversion and the Roth IRA then doubles in value over the next 10 years, you could look at your situation as only having paid 12.5 percent tax.

The prospect of tax-advantaged income is a tempting one. While you have to pay a conversion tax to transfer your assets, you also have turned taxable income into tax free retirement money that you can let grow as long as you want without being required to withdraw it. Your financial professional will likely tell you that it is not a matter of whether or not you should perform a Roth IRA conversion, it is a matter of how much you should convert and when.

Here are some of the things to consider before converting to a Roth IRA:

- If you make a conversion before you retire, you may end up paying higher taxes on the conversion because it is likely that you are in some of your highest earning years, placing you in the highest tax bracket of your life. It is possible that a better strategy would be to wait until after you retire, a time when you may have less taxable income, which would place you in a lower tax bracket.

- Many people opt to reduce their work hours from full-time to part-time in the years before they retire. If you have pursued this option, your income will likely be lower, in turn lowering your tax rate.

- The first years that you draw Social Security benefits can also be years of lower reported income, making it another good time frame in which to convert to a Roth IRA.

One key strategy to handling a Roth IRA conversion is to ***always be able to pay the cost of the tax conversion with outside money***. Structuring your tax year to include something like a significant deduction can help you offset the conversion tax. This way you aren't forced to take the money you need for taxes from the value of the IRA. The reason taxes apply to this maneuver is because when you withdraw money from a traditional IRA, it is treated as taxable income by the IRS. Your financial professional, with the help of the CPAs at their firm, may be able to provide you with options like after-tax money, itemized deductions or other situations that can pose effective tax avoidance options.

Some examples of avoiding Roth IRA conversions taxes include:

- *Using medical expenses that are above 10 percent of your Adjusted Gross Income.* If you have health care costs that you can list as itemized deductions, you can convert an amount of income from a traditional IRA to a Roth IRA that is offset by the deductible amount. Essentially, deductible medical expenses negate the taxes resulting from recording the conversion.

- *Individuals, usually small business owners, who are dealing with a Net Operating Loss (NOL).* If you have NOLs, but aren't able to utilize all of them on your tax return. You can carry them forward to offset the taxable income from the taxes on income you convert to a Roth IRA.

- *Charitable giving.* If you are charitably inclined, you can use the amount of your donations to reduce the amount of taxable income you have during that year. By matching the amount you convert to a Roth IRA to the amount your taxable income was reduced by charitable giving, you can essentially avoid taxation on the conversion. You may decide to double your donations to a charity in one year, giving them two years' worth of donations in order to offset the Roth IRA conversion tax on this year's tax return.

- *Investments that are subject to depletion.* Certain investments can kick off depletion expenses. If you make an investment and are subject to depletion expenses, they can be deducted and used to offset a Roth IRA conversion tax.

Not all of the above scenarios will work for everyone, but there are many other options for offsetting conversion taxes. The point is that you have options, and your financial professional and tax professional can help you understand those options.

If you have a traditional IRA, Roth conversions are something you should look at. As you approach retirement you should consider your options and make choices that keep more of your money in your pocket, not the government's.

Not only do Roth IRAs provide you with tax-advantaged growth, they also give you a tax diversified landscape that allows you to maximize your distributions. Chances are that no matter the circumstances, you will have taxed income and other assets subject to taxation. ***But if you have a Roth IRA, you have the unique ability to manage your Adjusted Gross Income (AGI), because you have a tax-advantaged income option!***

Converting to a Roth IRA can also help you preserve and build your legacy. Because Roth IRAs are exempt from RMDs, after you make a conversion from a traditional IRA, your Roth account can grow tax-advantaged for another 15, 20 or 25 years and it can be used as tax-advantaged income by your heirs. It is important to note, however, that non-spousal beneficiaries do have to take RMDs from a Roth IRA, or choose to stretch it and draw tax-advantaged income out of it over their lifetime.

TO CONVERT OR NOT TO CONVERT?

Conversions aren't only for retirees. You can convert at any time. Sticking with a traditional IRA or converting to a Roth depends on your individual circumstances, including your income, your tax bracket and the amount of deductions you have each year. Not everyone needs the tax benefits a Roth IRA provides, which makes an IRA a perfectly suitable option for their situation. For example, their income might not be very high and their RMD might not bump their tax bracket up, so it's not as big a deal. A similar situation might involve income from Social Security. Social Security benefits are taxed based on other income you are drawing. If you are in a position where none or very little of your Social Security benefit is subject to taxes, paying income tax on your RMD may be very easy. There are also situations where leveraging taxable income from a traditional IRA can work to your advantage come tax time.

> » *Caleb and Hannah dreamed of buying a boat when they retire. It is something they have looked forward to their entire marriage. In addition to the savings and investments that they created to supply them with income during retirement, which includes a traditional IRA, they have also saved money for the sole purpose of purchasing their dream boat once they stop working.*
>
> *When the time comes and they finally buy the boat of their dreams, they pay an additional $10,000 in sales taxes that year because of the large purchase. Because they are retired and earning less money, the deductions they used to be able to realize from their income taxes are no longer there. The high amount of sales taxes they paid on the boat puts them in a position where they could benefit from taking taxable income from a traditional IRA.*
>
> *When Caleb and Hannah's financial professional learns about their purchase, he immediately contacts a CPA at his firm to run the numbers. They determine that by taking a $10,000 distribution from their IRA, they could fulfill their income needs to offset the $10,000 sales tax deduction that they were claiming due to the purchase of their boat. In the end, they pay zero taxes on their income distribution from their IRA.*

The moral of the story? When you plan your taxes and have a tax diversified landscape, you create opportunities for yourself that would otherwise never have been possible. By having a robust combination of tax-advantaged income options, capital assets that can be liquidated, and holdings that can be used to create capital gains or losses, you put yourself in a position to play your cards right no matter what you want to accomplish with your taxes. The ace up your sleeve is your financial professional and the CPAs they work with.

Planning your taxes allows you to be creative and make the retirement plan right for you. You don't have to follow the herd and settle for a retirement strategy that doesn't satisfy your needs. If a traditional IRA or 401(k) isn't working for you, but converting to a Roth IRA or Roth 401(k) doesn't appeal to you, you still have options. **With proper planning, you can turn your IRA into a tax-free account by using a strategic roll-out.**

Essentially, a strategic roll-out involves repositioning the funds within your IRA so you can manage their tax implications at your own pace and then roll them out into a financial vehicle that allows for the tax-free accumulation, distribution, and transfer of funds. There are a variety of different methods you can use to offset the taxes that are usually triggered when you withdraw income from your IRA. In other words, by working with your financial professional you can create a strategy that will let you take money out of your IRA with little or no taxable consequence and reposition it within a tax-free vehicle, like a permanent life insurance policy. If done correctly, this option can be cheaper than converting to a Roth account and it will provide you with tax-free retirement income and your heirs with a tax-free inheritance! Taxes impact nearly every facet of your financial life, but they shouldn't control it. If you plan accordingly, you can design a purposeful, comprehensive, and easy to understand plan that will support you and your family for as long you need.

CHAPTER 8 RECAP //

- No retirement or legacy plan is complete if you have not yet developed and implemented a proactive tax strategy.

- The more money you keep, the more money you have that can be leveraged as an asset to maximize your financial potential.

- Creating a proactive tax strategy begins with having a tax-diversified portfolio and planning your taxes at the end of the taxable year, rather than just filling them at the beginning of the next one, so you can make decisions that will impact your tax return before you file it.

- Working with a financial professional is the best way to create the most beneficial tax plan.

- Retirement isn't the only stage of your life that can be unduly impacted by taxation: your estate and assets will both be subjected to taxes even after you're gone so make sure you have a plan in place that will allow your loved ones to receive your last gifts, instead of the government.

- Take control of your retirement accounts by rolling over your 401(k) into an IRA or Roth IRA.

- You can use a strategic roll-out to turn your IRA into a tax-free retirement account.

9

MAKING A PLAN ABOUT MORE THAN DOLLARS AND CENTS

If you're like most people, planning your estate isn't on the top of your list of things to do. Planning your income needs for retirement, managing your assets and just living your life without worrying about how your estate will be handled when you are gone make legacy planning less than attractive for a Saturday afternoon task. The fact of the matter, however, is that if you don't plan your legacy, someone else will. That someone else is usually a combination of the IRS and other government entities: lawyers, executors, courts, and accountants. Who do you think has the best interests of your beneficiaries in mind?

Today, there is more consideration given to planning a legacy than just maximizing your estate. When most people think about an estate, it may seem like something only the very wealthy have: a stately manor or an enormous business. But a legacy is something else entirely. A legacy is more than the sum total of the financial assets you have accumulated. It is the lasting impression you make on those you leave behind. The dollar and cents are just a small part of a legacy.

A legacy encompasses the stories that others tell about you, shared experiences and values. An estate may pay for college tuition, but a legacy may inform your grandchildren about the importance of higher education and self-reliance.

A legacy may also contain family heirlooms or items of emotional significance. It may be a piece of art your great-grandmother painted, family photos, or a childhood keepsake.

When you go about planning your legacy, certainly explore strategies that can maximize the financial benefit to the ones you care about. But also take the time to ensure that you have organized the whole of your legacy, part of the last gift you leave.

Many people avoid planning their legacy until they feel they must. Something may change in your life, like the birth of a grandchild, the diagnosis of a serious health problem, or the death of a close friend or loved one. Waiting for tragedy to strike in order to get your affairs in order is not the best course of action. The emotional stress of that kind of situation can make it hard to make patient, thoughtful decisions. Taking the time to create a premeditated and thoughtful legacy plan will assure that your assets will be transferred where and when you want them when the time comes.

THE BENEFITS OF PLANNING YOUR LEGACY

Eventually, when your income need is filled and you have sufficient standby money to meet your need for emergencies, travel or other extra expenses you are planning for, whatever isn't used during your lifetime becomes your financial legacy. The money that you do not use during your lifetime will either go to loved ones, unloved ones, charity, or the IRS. The questions is, who would you rather disinherit?

By having a legacy plan that clearly outlines your assets, your beneficiaries and your distribution goals, you can make sure that your money and property is ending up in the hands of the people you determine beforehand. Is it really that big of a deal? It absolutely is. Think about it. Without a clear plan, it is impossible for anyone to know if your beneficiary designations are current and reflect your wishes because you haven't clearly expressed who your beneficiaries are. You may have an idea of who you want your assets to go to, but without a plan, it is anyone's guess. It is also impossible to know if the titling of your assets is accurate unless you have gone through and determined whose name is on the titles.

As you can see, the distribution of your assets, whether they are in the form of property, stocks, Individual Retirement Accounts, 401(k)s or liquid assets, can be a complicated undertaking if you haven't left clear instructions about how you want them handled. Planning your legacy will help your assets be transferred with little delay and little confusion whereas not having a plan will cost more money and take more time, which means your loved ones will have to wait (sometimes for years) to receive less of your legacy than if you had a clear plan. Instead of leaving decisions about how to distribute your estate in the hands of your family, attorneys, or financial professionals, preserve your legacy and your wishes by drafting a clear plan at an early age. *By clearly and effectively communicating your desires regarding the planned distribution of your legacy, you protect your family from losing a large part of it.*

Unfortunately, as you have probably come to expect, the distribution of your estate is just as contaminated with taxes and unnecessary financial risk as a qualified account. Between taxes, Family Maximum Benefit calculations, probate, and a host of other issues, it should be apparent that managing your legacy is more complicated than having an attorney read your will, divide your estate and write checks to your heirs. Educating yourself about the best options for positioning your legacy assets is a challenging undertaking. Working with a financial professional who is well-versed in determining the most efficient and effective ways of preserving and distributing your legacy can save you time, money, and strife.

And while you know all that, it can still be hard to sit down and do it. It reminds you that life is short, and the relatively complicated nature of sorting through your assets can feel like a daunting task. Bear in mind, however, that there is more to your legacy beyond your property, money, investments and other assets that you leave to family members, loved ones and charities. You also leave behind personal items of importance, your values and beliefs, your personal and family history, and your dreams. Everyone has a legacy beyond money and it is equally as, if not more, important to make your wishes known to someone about how you want the rest of your personal legacy to be handled. When it comes time for your family and loved ones to make decisions after you are gone, knowing your wishes can help them make decisions that honor you and your legacy, and give meaning to what you leave behind. Without a plan, your legacy will just be a fragmented collection of financial, personal, and other more intangible assets. Give your loved ones the honor of seeing the whole beautiful picture.

Working with your financial professional will help you answer the hard questions and organize your estate and legacy. Ask yourself:

- Are the beneficiary designations on my assets up to date?
- Have my primary and contingent beneficiaries been clearly designated?
- Does my plan allow for restriction of a beneficiary?
- Does my legacy plan address minor children that I want to provide with income?
- Does my legacy plan allow for multi-generational payout?

- How do I want to pass on my personal legacy?
- What personal stories, values, and items of emotional significance do I want to impart and to whom?

Answers to these questions will help you create a plan that ensures your legacy is transferred and distributed to your loved ones in the manner you choose. Once you know what you want your legacy plan to accomplish, it's time to figure out what will actually be contained within your legacy. Sit down with your financial professional and create a detailed inventory of all your assets and any debts you may have. As you identify and list all of your assets, be sure to include how much they are worth, how they are titled and who the beneficiaries are. Your financial professional can then help you draft a plan that is in accordance with your wishes and will legally dictate how they should be distributed upon your death.

While this may seem like an overwhelming amount of information to consider and organize into a cohesive strategy, the good news is that if you already have a comprehensive and purposeful retirement plan in place, most of the hard work is already done. When you create a retirement plan that provides you with multiple sources of retirement income and protects you from undue taxation, it's not difficult for a well-structured legacy plan to follow.

CHAPTER 9 RECAP //

- If you don't plan your legacy, someone else will. To make sure that your assets are distributed in the way you would want, you need to create a legacy plan.
- Without a clear plan in place, you leave your legacy vulnerable to taxes and delays in its distribution.

- The first step towards creating your legacy plan is making a list of all your assets, as well as any debts you may have. Make sure the beneficiaries for each asset is up-to-date.
- Your legacy is more than the sum of your financial and material assets: it is the lasting impression you will leave on your loved ones. Having a plan in place helps to ensure that your legacy says exactly what you want it to.

10

LEAVING THE RIGHT LEGACY BEHIND

There are many potential tools you can use to ensure your legacy leaves the lasting message you want. If your primary concern is making sure your loved ones will be financially supported after you're gone, there is no better tool than our old friend, life insurance. By this point, you should be well-acquainted with the utility and benefits of life insurance, but it's important to highlight how these advantages can be used in a legacy-planning capacity. A good life insurance policy is one of the most powerful legacy tools you can leverage. Life insurance is a highly efficient legacy tool because it creates money when it is needed or desired the most. Over the years, life insurance has become less expensive, while it offers more features, and it provides longer guarantees.

LIFE INSURANCE: AN IMPORTANT LEGACY PLANNING TOOL

Life insurance is a useful and secure tool for contingency planning, ensuring that your dependents receive the assets that you want them to have, and for meeting the financial goals you have set for the future. While it bears the name "Life Insurance," it is, as you know, a diverse financial tool that can meet many needs. When the main function of a life insurance policy is to provide financial assets for your survivors, it is particularly well-suited to achieve this goal because it provides a tax-advantaged lump sum of money in the form of a death benefit to your beneficiary or beneficiaries.

Very few people want life insurance, but nearly everyone wants what it does. Life insurance is specifically, and uniquely, capable of creating money when it is needed most. When a loved one passes, no amount of money can remove the pain of loss. And certainly, money doesn't solve the challenges that might arise with losing someone important. But it has been said that when you have money, you have options. When you don't have money, your options are severely limited. You might imagine a life insurance policy can give your family and loved ones options that would otherwise be impossible.

> » *Alan spent the last 20 years building a small business. In so many ways, it is a family business. Each of his three children, Sarah, Nona and Chris, worked in the shop part-time during high school. But after all three attended college, only Nona returned to join her father, and eventually will run the business full-time when Alan retires.*
>
> *Alan is able to retire comfortably on Social Security and on-going income from the shop, but the business is nearly his entire financial legacy. It is his wish that Nona own the business outright, but he also wants to leave an equal legacy to each of his three children.*

> *There is no simple way to divide the business into thirds and still leave the business intact for Nona.*
> *Alan ends up buying a life insurance policy to make up the difference. Sarah and Chris will receive their share of an inheritance in cash from the life insurance policy and Nona will be able to inherit the business intact.*
> *Alan is able to accomplish his goals, treat all three children equitably and leave Nona the business she helped to build.*

As this example shows, the true beauty of a life insurance policy is that the financial asset it provides can be as flexible as you want it to be. This benefit can be structured in whichever way will help your beneficiaries get the most out of your legacy. Some of the available options include:

- Providing beneficiaries with a tax-free, liquid asset.
- Providing income for your dependents.
- Offering an investment opportunity for your beneficiaries.
- Covering expenses such as tuition or mortgage down payments for your children or grandchildren.
- Covering the costs associated with your death, including estate taxes.

In addition, using a life insurance policy can help you to *build* your legacy, not just protect it. Life insurance is one of the most surefire and efficient investment tools for building a substantial legacy that will meet your financial goals. If your Green Money income needs for retirement are met and you have Yellow Money assets that will provide for your future expenses, you may have extra assets that you want to earmark as legacy funds. By electing to invest those assets into a life insurance policy, you can immediately increase the amount of your legacy by providing your beneficiaries with an income tax-advantaged death benefit. What's more is that a good life insurance policy will also have the opportunity to accumulate in value over time and, should you require them, have an option to include long-term care (LTC) or chronic illness benefits.

An additional benefit is that life insurance is not considered to be part of the estate of the policy holder. The death benefit that is paid by the insurance company goes exclusively to the beneficiaries listed on the policy. This protects the proceeds of the policy from being chipped away at by attorneys' fees, probate proceedings costs, and claims made by creditors. The distribution of your life insurance policy is also unaffected by delays of the estate's distribution, like probate. Your beneficiaries will get the proceeds of the policy in a timely fashion, regardless of how long it takes for the rest of your estate to be settled.

Investing a portion of your assets in a life insurance policy can also protect that portion of your estate from creditors. If you owe money to someone or some entity at the time of your death, a creditor is not able to claim any money from a life insurance policy, or an annuity for that matter. An exception to this rule is if you had already used the life insurance policy as collateral against a loan. If a large portion of the money you want to dedicate to your legacy is sitting in a savings account, investment or other liquid form, creditors may be able to receive their claim on it before your beneficiaries get anything - that is, if there's anything left. A life insurance policy protects your assets from creditors and ensures that your beneficiaries get the money that you intend them to have.

LIFE INSURANCE AND TAXES

Tax liabilities on the estate you leave behind are inevitable. Capital property, for instance, is taxed at its fair market value at the time of your death, unless that property is transferred to your spouse. If the property has appreciated during the time you owned it, taxation on capital gains will occur. Registered Retirement Savings Plans (RRSPs) and other similarly structured assets are also included as taxable income unless transferred to a beneficiary as well. Those are just a few examples of how an estate can become subject to a heavy tax burden. The unique benefits of a life insurance policy provide ways to handle this tax burden, solving any liquidity problems that may arise if your family members want to hold onto an illiquid asset, such as a piece of property or an investment. Life insurance can provide a significant amount of money to a family member or other beneficiary, and that money is likely to remain exempt from taxation or seizure.

Life insurance allows you to transfer a tax-advantaged lump sum of money to your beneficiaries. It should come as no surprise that taxes can have a huge impact on your legacy. Not only that, income and assets from your legacy can have tax implications for your beneficiaries, as well.

Here's a brief overview of how taxes could affect your legacy and your beneficiaries:

- The higher your income, the higher the rate at which it is taxed.
- Withdrawals from qualified plans are taxed as income.
- What's more, when you leave a large qualified plan, it ends up being taxed at a high rate.
- If you left a $500,000 IRA to your child, they could end up owing as much as $140,000 in income taxes.
- However, if you could just withdraw $50,000 a year, the tax bill might only be $10,000 per year.

How could you use that annual amount to leave a larger legacy? Luckily, you can leverage a life insurance policy to avoid those tax penalties, preserving a larger amount of your legacy and freeing your beneficiaries from an added tax burden.

» *When Maria turned 75 years old, she decided it was time to look into life insurance policy options. She still feels young, but she remembers that her mother died in late 70s, and she wants to plan ahead so she can pass on some of her legacy to her grandchildren just like her grandmother did for her.*

Maria doesn't really want to think about life insurance, but she does want the security, reliability and tax-advantaged distribution that it offers. She lives modestly, and her Social Security benefit meets most of her income needs. As the beneficiary of her late husband's Certificate of Deposit (CD), she has $100,000 in an account that she has never used and doesn't anticipate ever needing since her income needs were already met.

*After looking at several different investment options with a professional, Maria decides that a Single Premium life insurance policy fits her needs best. She can buy the policy with a $100,000 one-time payment and she is guaranteed that it would provide more than the value of the contract to her beneficiaries. If she left the money in the CD, it would be subject to taxes. But for every dollar that she puts into the life insurance policy, her beneficiaries are guaranteed at least that dollar plus a death benefit, and all of it will be **tax-free!***

For $100,000, Maria's particular policy offers a $170,000 death benefit distribution to her beneficiaries. By moving the $100,000 from a CD to a life insurance policy, Maria increases her legacy by 70 percent. Not only that, she has also sheltered it from taxes, so her beneficiaries will be able to receive $1.70 for every $1.00 that she entered into the policy! While buying the policy doesn't allow her to use the money for herself, it does allow her family to benefit from her well-planned legacy.

MAKING IT WORK BY WORKING WITH A PROFESSIONAL

If you're like Maria and have waited to get a life insurance policy, speaking with a professional can show you its benefits. Determining the type of policy and the amount right for you depends on an analysis of your needs. Most people want there to be a formula that will tell them precisely what type and how much life insurance they should purchase. The truth of the matter is, however, that the answer will come from the individual. Ask yourself what you're hoping to accomplish with your policy: is it solely a legacy planning tool or would you also like to use it for retirement income? It's also important to think about how your age and health will affect the cost of your premiums.

A financial professional can help you complete a needs analysis that will highlight the amount of insurance that you require to meet your goals. This type of personalized review will allow you to determine ways to continue providing income for your spouse or any dependents you may have. A financial professional can also help you calculate the amount of income that your policy should replace to meet the needs of your beneficiaries and the duration of the distribution of that income.

You may also want to use your life insurance policy to meet any expenses associated with your death. These can include funeral costs, fees from probate and legal proceedings, and taxes. You may also want to dedicate a portion of your policy proceeds to help fund tuition or other expenses for your children or grandchildren. You can buy a policy and hope it covers all of those costs, or you can work with a professional who can calculate exactly how much insurance you need and how to structure it to meet your goals. Which would you rather do?

If you do, however, have a life insurance policy but haven't looked at it in a while, you may not know how it operates, how much it is worth and how it will be distributed to your beneficiaries. You may also need to update your beneficiaries on your policy. In short, without a comprehensive review of your policy, you don't really know where the money will go or to whom it will go.

The beneficiary designation of your life insurance supersedes your will's instruction. While there are benefits to having life insurance supersede the direction given in a will or other estate plan, it also poses some potential snags that you should address to make sure your wishes are met. For example, if your will instructs that your assets be divided equally between your two children but your life insurance beneficiary is listed as just one of the children, the assets in the life insurance policy will only be distributed to the child listed as the beneficiary. This is important to understand when designating beneficiaries on a policy you purchase. Work with a professional to make sure that your beneficiaries are accurately listed on your assets, especially your life insurance policies.

The importance of working with a trusted financial professional to help you either procure or review or your policy cannot be understated. Part of using life insurance to your greatest advantage is selecting the policy and provider that can best meet your goals. This requires the presence of a trusted financial professional who can help you cut through the red tape, the "sales-speak," and confusion to find a policy that meets your goals and best serves your desires for your money. If you already have a policy, a financial professional can help you review it and become familiar with the policy's premium, the guarantees the policy affords, its performance, its features, and its benefits. A financial professional can also help you make any necessary changes to the policy.

STRETCH IRAS: GETTING THE MOST OUT OF YOUR MONEY

A life insurance policy is not the only way to take care of your heirs after you're gone. A Stretch IRA is another strategy you can use that can help provide your kids and grandkids with a lifetime of income. In 1986, the U.S. Congress passed a law that allows for multi-generational distributions of IRA assets. This type of distribution is called a Stretch IRA because it stretches the distribution of the account out over a longer period of time to several beneficiaries. It also allows the account to continue accumulating value throughout your relatives' lifetimes. You can use a Stretch IRA as an income tool that distributes throughout your lifetime, your children's lifetimes and your grandchildren's lifetimes.

Stretch IRAs are an attractive option for those more concerned with creating income for their loved ones than leaving them with a lump sum that may be subject to a high tax rate. With traditional IRA distributions, non-spousal beneficiaries must generally take distributions from their inherited IRAs, whether transferred or not, within five years after the death of the IRA owner. An exception

Beneficiaries Stretch IRA Distributions

Beneficiaries FAIL to Stretch IRA Distributions

to this rule applies if the beneficiary elects to take distributions over his or her lifetime, which is referred to as stretching the IRA.

Let's begin by looking at the potential of stretching an IRA across multiple generations.

> *» Ted has an IRA with a current balance of $350,000. If we assume a five percent annual rate of return, and a 28% tax rate, the Stretch IRA turned a $502,625 legacy into more than $1.5 million. Doubling the value of the IRA also provided Ted, his wife, two children and three grandchildren with income. Not choosing the stretch option would have cost nearly $800,000 and had impacts on six of Ted's loved ones.*

Unfortunately, many things may also play a role in failing to stretch IRA distributions. It can be tempting for a beneficiary to take a lump sum of money despite the tax consequences. Fortunately, if you want to solidify your plan for distribution, there are options that will allow you to open up an IRA and incorporate "spendthrift" clauses for your beneficiaries. This will ensure your legacy is stretched appropriately and to your specifications. Only certain insurance companies allow this option, and you will not find this benefit with any brokerage accounts. You need to work with a financial professional who has the appropriate relationship with an insurance company that provides this option.

AVOIDING COMMON LEGACY PLANNING MISTAKES

Landry organized his assets long ago. He started planning his retirement early and made investment decisions that would meet his needs. With a combination of IRA to Roth IRA conversions, a series of income annuities and a well-planned money management strategy overseen by his financial professional, he easily filled his income gap and was able to focus on ways to accumulate his wealth throughout his retirement. He reorganized his I Know So Money and I Hope So Money as he got older.

When Landry retired, he had an income plan created that allowed him to maximize his Social Security benefit. He even had enough to accumulate wealth during his retirement. At this point, Landry turned his attention to planning his legacy. He wanted to know how he could maximize the amount of his legacy he will pass on to his heirs.

Landry met with an attorney to draw up a will, but he quickly learned that while having a will was a good plan, it wasn't the most efficient way to distribute his legacy. In fact, relying solely on a will created several issues..

The two main problems that arose for Landry were *Probate* and *Unintentional Disinheritance:*

Problem #1: Probate

Probate. Just speaking the word out loud can cause shivers to run down your spine. Probate's ugly reputation is well deserved. It can be a costly, time consuming process that diminishes your estate and can delay the distribution of your estate to your loved ones. Nasty stuff, by any measure. Unless you have made a clear legacy plan and discussed options for avoiding probate, it is highly likely that you have many assets that might pass through probate needlessly. ***If your will and beneficiary designations aren't correctly structured, some of these assets will go through the probate process, which can turn dollars into cents.***

If you have a will, probate is usually just a formality. There is little risk that your will won't be executed per your instructions. The problem arises when the costs and lengthy timeline that probate creates come into play. Probate proceedings are notoriously expensive, lengthy and ponderous. A typical probate process identifies all of your assets and debts, pays any taxes and fees that you owe (including estate tax), pays court fees, and distributes your property and assets to your heirs. This process usually takes at least a year, and can take even longer before your heirs actually receive anything that you have left for them. For this reason, and because of the sometimes exorbitant fees that may be charged by lawyers and accountants during the process, probate has earned a nasty reputation.

Probate can also be a strenuous public process. Because the probate process happens in court, the assets you own that go through a probate procedure become part of the public record. While this may not seem like a big deal to some, other people don't want that kind of intimate information available to the public.

Additionally, if your estate is entirely distributed via your will, the money that your family may need to cover the costs of your medical bills, funeral expenses and estate taxes will be tied up in probate, which can last up to a year or more. While immediate family members may have the option of requesting immediate cash from your assets during probate to cover immediate health care expenses, taxes, and fees, that process comes with its own set of complications. Choosing alternative methods for distributing your legacy can make life easier for your loved ones and can help them claim more of your estate in a more timely fashion than traditional methods.

A simpler and less tedious approach is to avoid probate altogether by structuring your estate to be distributed outside of the probate process. Two common ways of doing this are by structuring your assets inside a life insurance plan or by using individual retirement planning tools like IRAs that give you the option of designating a beneficiary upon your death.

Problem #2: Unintentionally Disinheriting Your Family

You would never want to unintentionally disinherit a loved one or loved ones because of confusion surrounding your legacy plan. Unfortunately, it happens. Why? This terrible situation is typically caused by a simple lack of understanding. In particular, mistakes regarding legacy distribution occur with regards to those whom people care for the most: their grandchildren.

One of the most important ways to plan for the inheritance of your grandchildren is by properly structuring the distribution of your legacy. Specifically, you need to know if your legacy is going to be distributed *per stirpes* or *per capita*.

Per Stirpes. *Per stirpes* is a legal term in Latin that means "by the branch." Your estate will be distributed *per stirpes* if you designate each branch of your family to receive an equal share of your estate. In the event that your children predecease you, their share will be distributed evenly between their children — your grandchildren.

Per Capita. *Per capita* distribution is different in that you may designate different amounts of your estate to be distributed to members of the same generation.

Per stirpes distribution of assets will follow the family tree down the line as the predecessor beneficiaries pass away. On the other hand, per capita distribution of assets ends on the branch of the family tree with the death of a designated beneficiary. For example, when your child passes away, in a per capita distribution, your grandchildren would not receive distributions from the assets that you designated to your child.

A simple way to remember the difference between the two types of distribution goes something like this: "***Stripes are forever and Capita is capped.***"

What the terms mean is not nearly as important as what they do, however. The reality is that improperly titled assets could accidentally leave your grandchildren disinherited upon the death of their parents. It's easy to check, and it's even easier to fix. Your financial professional can help make sure all of your assets are properly titled and, equally as important, check that all their beneficiaries are up-to-date so that you're not creating an unintentional heir.

> *When Helena turned 85, her daughter finally convinced her to meet with a financial professional to help her organize her assets and get her legacy in order. Although Helena was reluctant to let a stranger review her personal finances, she ended up being very glad that she did.*
>
> *In the process of listing Helena's assets and her beneficiaries, her professional finds a man's name listed as the beneficiary of an old annuity that she owns. It turns out that the man is Helena's ex-husband who is still alive. Had Helena passed away before her ex-husband, the annuities and any death benefits that came with them, would have been passed on to her ex-husband. This does not reflect her latest wishes.*

Our lives are in a constant state of transition as our relationships and circumstances evolve, so it's important that we periodically revisit our legacy plans and adapt them to reflect these changes in our lives. Maybe there is a new child or grandchild in your family that needs to be included or you have a new spouse to add or an old one to remove. Or perhaps the purpose that you created a particular account to fulfill has changed over the years and it's simply time to find a better way to leverage that account so it can meet a new purpose. A professional will regularly review your legacy assets and ask you questions to make sure that everything is up to date and that its current organization reflects your current wishes.

CHAPTER 10 RECAP //

- Organizing your estate will allow you to make sure your wishes are properly carried through.

- You can structure your assets in ways that maximize distributions to your beneficiaries.

- Working with a financial professional can help ensure that many of your assets avoid the ponderous and expensive probate process.

- A financial professional can help review the details of the assets you have designated to be a part of your legacy and make sure that you aren't unintentionally disinheriting your heirs or creating an accidental heir.

- Life insurance provides the distribution of tax-free, liquid assets to your beneficiaries.

- Investing in a life insurance policy can significantly build your legacy.

- Working with a financial professional can help you select the life insurance policy that best meets your needs, or he or she can help you fine tune your existing policy to better reflect your desires and intentions.

- You can take advantage of a "Stretch IRA" to provide income for you, your spouse and your beneficiaries throughout their lifetimes.

- Decide if you want your assets to be distributed *per stirpes* or *per capita*. Per stirpes distribution means each branch of your family tree will receive the same share of your estate and the assets will trickle down the family tree if a predecessor beneficiary passes away before you. Per capita distribution, on the other hand, allows you to give different amounts to each branch but those assets will not be passed down the line if the designated beneficiary predeceases you.

11

CHOOSING A FINANCIAL PROFESSIONAL

From the moment you dip your toes into the retirement planning pool to the point you start swimming laps, your assets organized, your income needs met, and your accumulation and legacy plans in place, working with a professional that you trust can make all the difference in how well your retirement reflects your desires.

It is important to know what you are looking for before taking the plunge. There are many people that would love to handle your money, but not everyone is qualified to handle it in a way that leads to a holistic approach to creating a solid retirement plan.

The distinction being made here is that you should look for someone that puts your interests first and actively wants to help you meet your goals and objectives. At times, the products someone sells you matter less than their dedication to making sure that you have a plan that meets your needs.

Professionals take your whole financial position into consideration. They make plans that adjust your risk exposure, invest in tools that secure your desired income during retirement and create investment strategies that allow you to continue accumulating wealth during your retirement for you to use later or to contribute to your legacy. If you buy stocks with a broker, use a different agent for a life insurance policy and have an unmanaged 401(k) through your employer, working with a financial professional will consolidate the management of your assets so you have one trustworthy person quarterbacking all of the team elements of your portfolio.

Financial products and investment tools change, but the concepts that lie behind wise retirement planning are lasting. In the end, you want to select a financial professional who is a complete advisor: someone who will take a holistic view of the needs of your situation and help you design a purposeful plan to address them. A successful retirement plan will consist of carefully selected investment and insurance products that operate within a unified a tax strategy. **You don't want to end up with a transactional advisor, someone who is more concerned with making a sale than making a plan.** In the end, you need an advisor who is not driven towards onlyf one product or strategy because that's what they know. You need someone who will work with you to create a thorough and diverse plan that you can understand and explain.

It's easy to see how choosing a financial professional can be one of the most important decisions you can make in your life. Not only do they provide you with advice, they also manage the personal assets that supply your retirement income and contribute to your legacy. So, how do you find a good one?

HOW TO FIND A FINANCIAL PROFESSIONAL YOU CAN TRUST

Taking care to select a financial professional is one of the best things you can do for yourself and for your future. Your professional has influence and control of your investment decisions, making their role in your life more than just important. Your financial security and the quality of your retirement depends on the decisions, investment strategies and asset structuring that you and your professional create.

Working with a professional is different than calling up a broker when you want to buy or trade some stock. This isn't a decision that you can hand off to anyone else. You need to bring your time and attention to the table when it comes to finding someone with whom you can entrust your financial life. Separating the wheat from the chaff will take some work, but you'll be happy you did it.

While no one can tell you exactly who to choose or how to choose them, the following information can help you narrow the field:

You can start by asking your friends, family and colleagues for referrals. You will want to pay particular attention to the recommendations that you get from others who are in your similar financial situation and who have similar lifestyle choices. The professional for the CEO of your company may have a different skill-set than the skill-set of the professional befitting your cousin who has 3 kids and a Subaru like you. Do follow-up research on the Internet as well. Look up the people who have been recommended to you on websites like LinkedIn that show the work history, referrals and experience of the candidates that you find most attractive. You will also learn about the firms with or for whom they work. The investment philosophies and reputations of the companies they work for will tell you a lot about how they will handle your money.

The other side of the coin, however, is that everyone and their brother has a recommendation about how you should manage your money and who should manage it for you. From hot stock tips to "the best money manager in the state," people love to share good information that makes them look like they are in-the-know. Nobody wants to talk about the bad stock purchases they made, the times they lost money and the poor selections they made regarding financial professionals or stock brokers. If you decide to take a friend or family member's recommendation, make sure they have a substantial, long-term experience with the financial professional and that their glowing review isn't just based on a one-time "win."

You can also use online tools like the search function of the Financial Planning Association (http://www.fpanet.org/) and the National Association of Personal Financial professionals (http://www.napfa.org/). Most of the professionals listed on these sites do not earn commissions from selling financial products, but are instead paid on a fee-only basis for their services. It is important to understand how your professional is being paid. It is generally considered preferable to work with a fee-based professional who will not have conflicts of interests between earning a commission and acting in your best interests.

Many professionals may also be brokers or dealers that can earn commissions on things like life insurance, certain types of annuities and disability insurance. These professionals have most likely intentionally overlapped their roles so that if their clients choose to purchase insurance or investment products that require a broker or dealer, those clients won't have to find an additional person to work with. Again, understanding the role of your professional will help you make your determination.

NARROWING THE FIELD
1. Decide on the Type of Professional with Whom You Want to Work. There are four basic kinds of financial professionals. Many

professionals may play overlapping roles. It is important to know a professional's primary function, how they charge for their services and whether they are obligated to act in your best interest.

Registered representatives, better known as stockbrokers or bank/investment representatives, make their living by earning commissions on insurance products and investment services. Stockbrokers basically sell you things. The products from which they make the highest commission are sometimes the products that they recommend to their clients. If you want to make a simple transaction, such as buying or selling a particular stock, a registered representative can help you. Although registered representatives are licensed professionals, if you want to create a structured and simple approach to positioning your assets for retirement, you might want to consider continuing your search.

The term "planner" is often misused. It can refer to credible professionals that are CPAs, CFPs and ChFCs to your uncle's next door neighbor who claims to have a lead on some undervalued stock about to be "discovered." A wide array of people may claim to be planners because there are no requirements to be a planner. The term financial planner, however, refers to someone who is properly registered as an investment advisor and serves as a fiduciary as described below.

Financial professionals are the diamonds in the rough. These Registered Investment Advisors are compensated on a fee basis. They do, however, often have licensure as stockbrokers or insurance agents, allowing them to earn commissions on certain transactions. More importantly, **financial professionals are financial fiduciaries, meaning they are required to make financial decisions in your best interest and reflecting your risk tolerance.** Investment Advisors are held to high ethical standards and are highly regarded in the financial industry. Financial professionals also often take a more comprehensive approach to asset management. These professionals are trained and credentialed to plan and coordinate their clients' assets in order to meet their goals or retirement and legacy planning. They are not focused on individual stocks, investments or markets. They look at the big picture, the whole enchilada.

Money managers are on par with financial professionals. However, they are often given explicit permission to make investment decisions without advanced approval by their clients.

Understanding who you are working with and what their title is the first step to planning your retirement. While each of the above-mentioned types of financial professionals can help you with aspects of your finances, it is **financial professionals** who have the most intimate role, the most objective investment strategies and the most unbiased mode of compensation for their services. A financial professional can also help you with the non-financial aspects of your legacy and can help you find ways to create a tax planning strategy to help you save money.

2. Be Objective. At the end of the day, you need to separate the weak from the strong. While you might want a strong personal rapport with your professional, or you may want to choose your professional for their personality and positive attitude, it is more important that you find someone who will give sage advice regarding achieving your retirement goals.

It can be helpful to use a process of elimination to narrow the field of potential professionals. Look into five or six potential leads and cross off your list the ones that don't meet your requirements until only one or two remain. Cross-check your remaining choices against the list of things you need from a professional. Make sure they represent a firm that has the investment tools and products that you desire, and make sure they have experience in retirement planning. That is, after all, the main goal.

Don't be afraid to investigate each of your candidates. You'll want to ask the same questions and look for the same information from everyone you consider so you can then compare them and decide which is best for you. You'll want to take a look at the specific credentials of each professional, their experience and competence, their ethics and fiduciary status, their history and track record, and a list of the services that they offer. The professionals who meet all or most of your qualifications are the ones you will contact for an interview.

Potential professionals should meet your qualifications in the following categories:

- *Credentials:* Look at their experience, the quality of their education, any associations to which they belong and certifications they have earned. Someone who has continued their professional education through ongoing certifications will be more up-to-date on current financial practices compared to someone who got their degree 25 years ago and hasn't done a thing since.
- *Practices:* Look at the track record of your candidates, how they are compensated for their services, the reports and analysis they offer, and their value added services.
- *Services:* Your professional must meet your needs. If you are planning your retirement, you should work with someone who offers services that help you to that end. You want someone who can offer planning, advice on investment strategies, ways to calculate risk, advice on insurance and annuities products, and ways to manage your tax strategy.
- *Ethics:* You want to work with someone who is above board and does things the right way. Select them by checking their compliance record, current licensing, fiduciary status and, yes, even their criminal record. You never know!

3. Ask for and Check References. Once you have selected two or three professionals that you want to meet, call or email them and ask for references. Every professional should be able to provide you with at least two or three names. In fact, they will probably be eager to share them with you. Most professionals rely on references for validation of their success, quality of services and likability. You should, however, take them with a grain of salt. You have no way to know whether or not references are a professional's friends or colleagues.

It is worth contacting references, however, to check for inconsistencies. Ask each reference the same set of questions to get the same basic information. How long have they been working with the professional? What kind of services have they used and were they happy with them? What type of financial planning did they use the professional for? Were they versed in the type of financial planning that you needed? You can also ask them direct questions to elicit candid responses. What was the full cost of the expenses that your professional charged you? Do the reports and statements you receive come from the same firm? Questions like these can help you get a sense of how well the reference knows their professional and whether or not they are a quality reference.

A good reference is a bit like icing on the cake. It's nice to have them, but nothing speaks louder than a good track record and quality experience. And remember that a good reference, while nice to hear, is relatively cheap. How many times have you heard someone on the golf course or at work telling you how great their stockbroker is? But how many times have you heard about the bad investments or losses they have experienced?

4. Use the Internet. As a final step before picking up the phone and calling your candidates, do some digging to discover if anyone on your list has a history of unlawful or unethical practices, or has been disciplined for any of their professional behavior or decisions. Don't worry, you don't have to hire a private investigator. You can easily find this information on the Financial Industry Regulatory

Authority's (FINRA) online BrokerCheck tool: http://www.finra. org/Investors/ToolsCalculators/BrokerCheck/.

You should obviously explore the website of a potential professional and the website of the firm that they represent. The Internet allows you to go beyond the online business card of a professional to gain access to information that they don't control. It may all be good information! Or a brief search of the Internet could reveal a sketchy past. The best part is that the Internet allows you to find helpful information in an anonymous fashion.

Start with Google (www.google.com) and search the name of a potential professional and their firm. Keep your eyes trained on third party sources such as articles, blog posts or news stories that mention the professional. You can also check a professional's compliance records online with the Financial Industry Regulatory Authority (FINRA) and the Securities and Exchange Commission (SEC). If you want to dig deeper, you can combine search terms like "scams," "lawsuits," "suspensions" and "fraud" with a professional's or firm's name to see what information arises. More likely than not, you won't find anything. But if you do, you'll be glad that you checked.

HOW TO INTERVIEW CANDIDATES

After selecting your candidates and narrowing down a list of professionals that you think might be a good fit for you, it's time to start interviewing.

When you meet in person with a professional, you want to take advantage of your time with them. The presentations and information that they share with you will be important to pay attention to, but you will also want to control some aspects of the interview. After a professional has told you what they want you to hear, it's time to ask your own questions to get the specific information you need to make your decision.

Make sure to prepare a list of questions and an informal agenda so that you can keep track of what you want to ask and what points you want the professional to touch on during the interview. Using the same questions and agenda will also allow you to more easily compare the professionals after you have interviewed them all. Remember that these interviews are just that, *interviews*. You are meeting with several professionals to determine with whom you want to work. Don't agree to anything or sign anything during an interview until after you have made your final decision.

It can also be helpful to put a time limit on your interviews and to meet the professionals at their offices. The time limit will keep things on track and will allow structured time for presentations and questions/discussion. By meeting them at their office, you can get a sense of the work environment, the staff culture and attitude, and how the firm does business. If you are unable to travel to a professional's office and must meet them at your home or office, make sure that your interviews are scheduled with plenty of time between so the professionals don't cross each other's paths.

You can use the following questions during an initial interview to get an understanding of how each professional does business and whether they are a good fit for you:

1. How do you charge for your services? How much do you charge? This information should be easy to find on their website, but if you don't see it, ask. Find out if they charge an initial planning fee, if they charge a percentage for assets under their management and if they make money by selling specific financial products or services. If so, you should follow up by asking how much the service costs. This will give you an idea of how they really make their money and if they have incentive to sell certain products over others. Make sure you understand exactly how you will be charged so there are no surprises down the road if you decide to work with this person.

2. What are your credentials, licenses, and certifications? There are Certified Financial Planners (CFPs), Chartered Financial Consultants (ChFCs), Investment Advisor Representatives, Certified Public Accountants (CPAs) and Personal Financial Specialists (PFSs). Whatever their credentials or titles, you want to be sure that the professional you work with is an expert in the field relevant to your circumstances. If you want someone to manage your money, you will most likely look for an Investment Advisor. Someone that works with an independent firm will likely have a team of CPAs, CFPs and other financial experts upon whom they can draw. If you like the professional you are meeting with and you think they might be a good fit, but they don't have the accounting experience you want them to have, ask them about their firm and the resources available to them. If they work closely with CPAs that are experienced in your needs, it could be a good match.

3. What are the financial services that you and your firm provide? The question within the question here is, "Can you help me achieve my goals?" Some people can only provide you with investment advice, and others are tax consultants. You will likely want to work with someone that provides a complete suite of financial planning services and products that touch on retirement planning, insurance options, legacy and estate structuring, and tax planning. Whatever services they provide, make sure they meet your needs and your anticipated needs.

4. What kinds of clients do you work with the most? A lot of financial professionals work within a niche: retirement planning, risk assessment, life insurance, etc. Finding someone who works with other people that are in the same financial boat as you and who have similar goals can be an important way to make sure they understand your needs. While someone might be a crackerjack annuities cowboy, you might not be interested in that option. Ask follow-up questions that will really help you understand where their expertise lies and whether or not their experience lines up with your needs.

5. May I see a sample of one of your financial plans? You wouldn't buy a car without test driving it, and you should not work with a professional without seeing a sample of how they do business. While there is no formal structure that a financial plan has to follow, the variation between professionals can help you find someone who "speaks your language." One professional may provide you with an in-depth analysis that relies heavily on info graphics and diagrams. Someone else may give you a seven page review of your assets and general recommendations. By seeing a sample plan, you can narrow down who presents information in the way that you desire and in ways that you understand.

6. How do you approach investing? You may be entirely in the dark about how to approach your investments, or you might have some guiding principles. Either way, ask each candidate what their philosophy is. Some will resonate with you and some won't. A good professional who has a realistic approach to investing won't promise you the moon or tell you that they can make you a lot of money. Professionals who are successful at retirement planning and full service financial management will tell you that they will listen to your goals, risk tolerance and comfort level with different types of investment strategies. Working with someone that you trust is critical, and this question in particular can help you find out who you can and who you can't.

7. How do you remain in contact with your clients? Does your prospective professional hold annual, quarterly or monthly meetings? How often do *you* want to meet with your professional? Some people want to check in once a year, go over everything and make sure their ducks are all in a row. If any changes over the previous year or additions to their legacy planning strategy came up, they'll do it on that date. Other people want a monthly update to be more involved in the decision making process and to understand what's happening with their portfolio. You basically need to determine the right degree of involvement for both you and your financial professional. You'll also want to feel out how your professional communicates. Do you prefer phone calls or face-to-face meetings? Do you want your professional to explain things to you in detail or to summarize for you what recommendations they've made? Is the professional willing to give you their direct phone number or their email address? More importantly, do you want that information and do you want to be able to contact them in those ways?

8. Are you my main contact, or do you work with a team? This is another way of finding out how involved with you your professional will be, and how often they will meet with you. It is also a way to discover how the firm they represent operates and manages their clients. Some professionals will answer their own phone, meet with you regularly and have your home phone number on speed dial. Others will meet with you once a year and have a partner or assistant check in with you every quarter to give you an update. Other companies take an entirely team-based approach whereby clients have a main contact but their portfolio is handled by a team of professionals that represent the firm. One way isn't better than another, but one way will be best for you. Find out how the professional you are interviewing operates before entering into an agreement.

9. How do you provide a unique experience for your clients? This is a polite way of asking, "Why should I work with you?" A professional should have a compelling answer to this question that connects with you. Their answer will likely touch on their investment philosophy, their communication style and their expertise. If you hear them describing strengths and philosophies that resonate with you, keep them on your list. Some professionals will tell you that they will make investments with your money that match your values, others will say they will maximize your returns and others will say they will protect your capital while structuring your assets for income. Whatever you're looking for in a professional, you will most likely find it in the answer to this question.

This last question you will want to ask *yourself* after you've met with someone who you are considering hiring:

10. Did they ask questions and show signs that they were interested in working with me? A professional who will structure your assets to reflect your risk tolerance and to position you for a comfortable retirement must be a good listener. You will want to pass by a professional who talks nonstop and tells you what to do without listening to what you want them to do. If you felt they listened well and understood your needs, and seemed interested and experienced in your situation, then they might be right for you.

THE IMPORTANCE OF INDEPENDENCE

Not all investment firms and financial professionals are created equal. The information in this book has systematically shown that leveraging investments for income and accumulation in today's market requires new ideas and modern planning. In short, you need innovative ideas to come up with the creative solutions that will provide you with the retirement that you want. Innovation thrives on independence. No matter how good a financial professional is, the firm that they represent needs to operate on principles that make sense in today's economy. Remember, advice about money has been around forever. Good advice, however, changes with the times.

Timing the market, relying on the sale of stocks for income and banking on high treasury and bond returns are not strategies. They aren't even realistic ways to make money or to generate income. Working with an independent agent can help you break free from the old ways of thinking and position you to create a realistic retirement plan.

Working with an independent professional who relies on fee-based income tied to the success of their performance will also give you greater peace of mind. When you do well, they do well, and that's the way it should be. Your independent financial professional will make sure that:

- Your assets are organized and structured to reflect your risk tolerance.
- Your assets will be available to you when you need them and in the way that you need them.
- You will have a lifetime income that will support your lifestyle through your retirement.
- You are handling your taxes as efficiently as possible.
- Your legacy is in order.
- Your Red Money is turned into Yellow Money, and is managed in your best interest.

» Remember Wallace and Mackenzie from Chapter 1? Even though they knew they had Social Security benefits coming, they placed some money in savings and Wallace had his pension and Mackenzie had her 401(k). **Before they met with a financial professional, they had no idea what their retirement would look like.** *After they met with a professional, they knew exactly what types of assets they had, how much they were worth, how much risk they were exposed to and how they were going to be distributed. They also created an income plan so*

that they could pay their bills every month the moment they retired, and they maximized their Social Security benefit by targeting the year and month they would get the most lifetime benefits. After their income needs were met, they were able to continue accumulating wealth by investing their extra assets to serve them in the future and contribute to their legacy. Their professional also helped them make decisions that impacted their taxes, protecting the value of their assets and allowing them to keep more of their money.

*This isn't a fairy tale scenario. This is an example of how much you stand to gain by meeting with a financial professional who can help you create a comprehensive, purposeful and easy to understand plan for your retirement. The concept of I Know So Money and I Hope So Money didn't just apply to their money, it also applied to Wallace and Mackenzie. They **hoped** that they would have enough for retirement and that they had worked hard enough and saved enough to maintain their lifestyle. Working with a financial professional allowed them to **know** that their income needs were secured and structured to provide them with income for the rest of their lives and with some money to spare.*

Now, ask yourself: Is your retirement built on hopes and dreams, or a solid, predictable plan?

IT'S WORTH IT!

Finding, interviewing and selecting a financial professional can seem like a daunting task. And honestly, it will take a good amount of work to narrow the field and find the one you want. In the end, it is worth the blood, sweat and tears. Your retirement, lifestyle, assets and legacy are on the line. The choices you make today will have lasting impacts on your life and the life of your loved ones. Working with someone you trust and know you can rely on to make decisions that will benefit you is invaluable. The work it takes to find them is something you will never regret.

Here is a recap of why working with a financial professional is the best retirement decision you can make:

CHAPTER 11 RECAP //

- If you feel you have more *I Hope So Money* than *I Know So Money* about your money and what your retirement is going to look like, working with a financial professional will give you clarity and confidence about what decisions are best for you.

- It is difficult for individual investors to not make emotional decisions about their investments. Financial professionals work with your risk tolerance, income needs and assets to find the most logical, efficient and beneficial way for you to structure your investments.

- As the DALBAR report showed, a majority of individual investors sell low when the market goes down and buy high when it goes back up. This is literally the exact opposite of what they should do to maximize their returns. Why? Emotions.

- A financial professional can help you change strategies when the market isn't going your way, but they won't abandon ship. They will stick to a simple approach. Your retirement isn't based on individual products or investments. It is based on a well-planned strategy that your financial professional is qualified to provide.

- Yellow Money is different from a mutual fund or a 401(k) because, while funds and 401(k)s are investment tools, they are not investment strategies. A 401(k) can be particularly misconceiving because your employer isn't truly structuring your investments inside the 401(k). They are simply providing you with a few options. The same goes for mutual funds.

They are not truly managed by someone who is obligated to have your best interests and your risk tolerance in mind. In fact, the investment strategies of mutual funds change on a regular basis, and you might not know about it until you get an annual report a *month* later.

- The biggest difference between working with a financial professional to manage your funds, and buying a mutual fund is that, while a mutual fund buys 20 stocks and pegs its earnings on the overall performance of the portfolio, a financial professional works with you to create an overall financial strategy that meets your needs. It may or may not include mutual funds.

- As an individual investor, do you really have an overarching strategy for your financial portfolio? How did you come up with your selections? Do you know how they are individually managed? Do you know how to make changes to your portfolio that reflect your risk tolerance? Do you know what your risk tolerance is?

- Managed money has a specific criteria and a professional will fit that into your overall financial plan so that it works the way you want it to.

- Not all investment firms and financial professionals are created equal. Working with an independent professional will give you more options that are customizable to your life.

ADDITIONAL RESOURCES

As part of their ongoing commitment to providing education and clarity to the retirement planning process, Robert and Chris Maggi created the following websites. They are invaluable resources to utilize as you begin mapping out your retirement future.

Help with Social Security:
Many people trigger their Social Security benefit at the wrong time. Don't be one of them! This website will provide you with the information and tools you need to know when and how to file so you can maximize your lifetime benefit.
www.planningmysocialsecurity.com

Help with Your Current Annuities:
If you currently have an annuity but you're not entirely confident it's the right one for you, it's time to re-evaluate. Making sure your past financial decisions are still in line with your current goals is always the right choice.
www.helpmyannuityplease.com

Help with Finding Your Tax-Free Income:
Since you first started earning a paycheck, having a tax-free income has probably always seemed like a dream, but what if it didn't have to be? This website will help guide you through the steps required to see if you can make that dream a reality and secure your retirement future.
www.ilovetaxfreeincome.com

Help with Everything Else:
If you have a need or question that isn't addressed through the use of one of these websites, it's best to go to the source.
www.maggitax.com

If you have a Brokerage Account:
Many clients are confused about the fees and loads in their account. This website will help you get an x-ray of your accounts. Stop paying unnecessary fees and high commissions.
www.xraymybrokerageaccount.com

Are you on Track for Retirement?
If you are not sure if you are on track for retirement or if you are in retirement and need help. Take the 10 question assestment and get answers to your questions.
www.maggifinancial.com

GLOSSARY

ANNUAL RESET *(ANNUAL RATCHET, CLIQUET)* – Crediting methods measuring index movement over a one year period. Positive interest is calculated and credited at the end of each contract year and cannot be lost if the index subsequently declines. Say that the index increased from 100 to 110 in one year and the indexed annuity had an 80 percent participation rate. The insurance company would take the 10 percent gross index gain for the year (110-100/100), apply the participation rate (10 percent index gain x 80 percent rate) and credit 8 percent interest to the annuity. But, what if in the following year the index declined back to 100? The individual would keep the 8 percent interest earned and simply receive zero interest for the down year. An annual reset structure preserves credited gains and treats negative index periods as years with zero growth.

ANNUITANT – The person, usually the annuity owner, whose life expectancy is used to calculate the income payment amount on the annuity.

ANNUITY – An annuity is a contract issued by an insurance company that often serves as a type of savings plan used by individuals looking for long term growth and protection of assets that will likely be needed within retirement.

AVERAGING – Index values may either be measured from a start point to an end point (point-to-point) or values between the start point and end point may be averaged to determine an ending value. Index values may be averaged over the days, weeks, months or quarters of the period.

BENEFICIARY – A beneficiary is the person designated to receive payments due upon the death of the annuity owner or the annuitant themselves.

BONUS RATE – A bonus rate is the "extra" or "additional" interest paid during the first year (the initial guarantee period), typically used as an added incentive to get consumers to select their annuity policy over another.

CALL OPTION *(ALSO SEE PUT OPTION)* – Gives the holder the right to buy an underlying security or index at a specified price on or before a given date.

CAP – The maximum interest rate that will be credited to the annuity for the year or period. The cap usually refers to the maximum interest credited after applying the participation rate or yield spread. If the index methodology showed a 20 percent increase, the participation rate was 60 percent and the maximum interest cap was 10 percent, the contract would credit 10 percent interest. A few annuities use a maximum gain cap instead of a maximum interest cap with the participation rate or yield spread applied to the lesser of the gain or the cap. If the index methodology showed a 20 percent increase, the participation rate was 60 percent and the maximum gain cap was 10 percent, the contract would credit 6 percent interest.

COMPOUND INTEREST – Interest is earned on both the original principal and on previously earned interest. It is more favorable than simple interest. Suppose that your original principal was $1 and your interest rate was 10 percent for five years. With simple interest, your value is ($1 + $0.10 interest each year) = $1.50. With compound interest, your value is ($1 x 1.10 x 1.10 x 1.10 x 1.10 x 1.10) = $1.61. The advantage of compound interest over simple interest becomes greater as each subsequent period passes.

CREDITING METHOD *(ALSO SEE METHODOLOGY)* – The formula(s) used to determine the excess interest that is credited above the minimum interest guarantee.

DEATH BENEFITS – The payment the annuity owner's estate or beneficiaries will receive if he or she dies before the annuity matures. On most annuities, this is equal to the current account value. Some annuities offer an enhanced value at death via an optional rider that has a monthly or annual fee associated with it.

EXCESS INTEREST – Interest credited to the annuity contract above the minimum guaranteed interest rate. In an indexed annuity the excess interest is determined by applying a stated crediting method to a specific index or indices.

FIXED ANNUITY – A contract issued by an insurance company guaranteeing a minimum interest rate with the crediting of excess interest determined by the performance of the insurer's general account. Index annuities are fixed annuities.

FIXED DEFERRED ANNUITY – With fixed annuities, an insurance company offers a guaranteed interest rate plus safety of your principal and earnings ((subject to the claims-paying ability of the insurance company). Your interest rate will be reset periodically, based on economic and other factors, but is guaranteed to never fall below a certain rate.

FREE WITHDRAWALS – Withdrawals that are free of surrender charges.

INDEX – The underlying external benchmark upon which the crediting of excess interest is based, also a measure of the prices of a group of securities.

IRA *(INDIVIDUAL RETIREMENT ACCOUNT)* – An IRA is a tax-advantaged personal savings plan that lets an individual set aside money for retirement. All or part of the participant's contributions may be tax deductible, depending on the type of IRA chosen and the participant's personal financial circumstances. Distributions from many employer-sponsored retirement plans may be eligible to be rolled into an IRA to continue tax-deferred growth until the funds are needed. An annuity can be used as an IRA; that is, IRA funds can be used to purchase an annuity.

IRA ROLLOVER – IRA rollover is the phrase used when an individual who has a balance in an employer-sponsored retirement plan transfers that balance into an IRA. Such an exchange, when properly handled, is a tax-advantaged transaction.

LIQUIDITY – The ease with which an asset is convertible to cash. An asset with high liquidity provides flexibility, in that the owner can easily convert it to cash at any time, but it also tends to decrease profitability.

MARKET RISK – The risk of the market value of an asset fluctuating up or down over time. In a fixed or fixed indexed annuity, the original principal and credited interest are not subject to market risk. Even if the index declines, the annuity owner would receive no less than their original principal back if they decided to cash in the policy at the end of the surrender period. Unlike a security, indexed annuities guarantee the original premium and the premium is backed by, and is as safe as, the insurance company that issued it (subject to the claims-paying ability of the insurance company).

METHODOLOGY *(ALSO SEE CREDITING METHOD)* – The way that interest crediting is calculated. On fixed indexed annuities, there are a variety of different methods used to determine how index movement becomes interest credited.

MINIMUM GUARANTEED RETURN *(MINIMUM INTEREST RATE)* – Fixed indexed annuities typically provide a minimum guaranteed return over the life of the contract. At the time that the owner chooses to terminate the contract, the cash surrender value is compared to a second value calculated using the minimum guaranteed return and the higher of the two values is paid to the annuity owner.

OPTION – A contract which conveys to its holder the right, but not the obligation, to buy or sell something at a specified price on or before a given date. After this given date the option ceases to exist. Insurers typically buy options to provide for the excess interest potential. Options may be American style whereby they may be exercised at any time prior to the given date, or they may have to be exercised only during a specified window. Options that may only be exercised during a specified period are European-style options.

OPTION RISK – Most insurers create the potential for excess interest in an indexed annuity by buying options. Say that you could buy a share of stock for $50. If you bought the stock and it rose to $60 you could sell it and net a $10 profit. But, if the stock price fell to $40 you'd have a $10 loss. Instead of buying the actual stock, we could buy an option that gave us the right to buy the stock for $50 at any time over the next year. The cost of the option is $2. If the stock price rose to $60 we would exercise our option, buy the stock at $50 and make $10 (less the $2 cost of the option). If the price of the stock fell to $40, $30 or $10, we wouldn't use the option and it would expire. The loss is limited to $2 – the cost of the option.

PARTICIPATION RATE – The percentage of positive index movement credited to the annuity. If the index methodology determined that the index increased 10 percent and the indexed annuity participated in 60 percent of the increase, it would be said that the contract has a 60 percent participation rate. Participation rates may also be expressed as asset fees or yield spreads.

POINT-TO-POINT – A crediting method measuring index movement from an absolute initial point to the absolute end point for a period. An index had a period starting value of 100 and a period ending value of 120. A point-to-point method would record a positive index movement of 20 [120-100] or a 20 percent positive movement [(120-100)/100]. Point-to-point usually refers to annual periods; however the phrase is also used instead of term end point to refer to multiple year periods.

PREMIUM BONUS – A premium bonus is additional money that is credited to the accumulation account of an annuity policy under certain conditions.

PUT OPTION *(ALSO SEE CALL OPTION)* – Gives the holder the right to sell an underlying security or index at a specified price on or before a given date.

QUALIFIED ANNUITIES *(QUALIFIED MONEY)* – Qualified annuities are annuities purchased for funding an IRA, 403(b) tax-deferred annuity or other type of retirement arrangements. An IRA or qualified retirement plan provides the tax deferral. An annuity contract should be used to fund an IRA or qualified retirement plan to benefit from an annuity's features other than tax deferral, including the safety features, lifetime income payout option and death benefit protection.

REQUIRED MINIMUM DISTRIBUTION *(RMD)* – The amount of money that Traditional, SEP and SIMPLE IRA owners and qualified plan participants must begin distributing from their retirement accounts by April 1 following the year they reach age 70.5. RMD amounts must then be distributed each subsequent year.

RETURN FLOOR – Another way of saying minimum guaranteed return.

ROTH IRA – Like other IRA accounts, the Roth IRA is simply a holding account that manages your stocks, bonds, annuities, mutual funds and CD's. However, future withdrawals (including earnings and interest) are typically tax-advantaged once the account has been open for five years and the account holder is age 59.5.

RULE OF 72 – Tells you approximately how many years it takes a sum to double at a given rate. It's handy to be able to figure out, without using a calculator, that when you're earning a 6 percent return, for example, by dividing 6 percent into 72, you'll find that it takes 12 years for money to double. Conversely, if you know it took a sum twelve years to double you could divide 12 into 72 to determine the annual return (6 percent).

SIMPLE INTEREST *(ALSO SEE <u>COMPOUND INTEREST</u>)* – Interest is only earned on the principal balance.

SPLIT ANNUITY – A split annuity is the term given to an effective strategy that utilizes two or more different annuity products – one designed to generate monthly income and the other to restore the original starting principal over a set period of time.

STANDARD & POOR'S 500 *(S&P 500)* – The most widely used external index by fixed indexed annuities. Its objective is to be a benchmark to measure and report overall U.S. stock market performance. It includes a representative sample of 500 common stocks from companies trading on the New York Stock Exchange, American Stock Exchange, and NASDAQ National Market System. The index represents the price or market value of the underlying stocks and does not include the value of reinvested dividends of the underlying stocks.

STOCK MARKET INDEX – A report created from a type of statistical measurement that shows up or down changes in a specific financial market, usually expressed as points and as a percentage, in a number of related markets, or in an economy as a whole (i.e. S&P 500 or New York Stock Exchange).

SURRENDER CHARGE – A charge imposed for withdrawing funds or terminating an annuity contract prematurely. There is no industry standard for surrender charges, that is, each annuity product has its own unique surrender charge schedule. The charge is usually expressed as a percentage of the amount withdrawn prematurely from the contract. The percentage tends to decline over time, ultimately becoming zero.

TRADITIONAL IRA – See <u>IRA (Individual Retirement Account)</u>

TERM END POINT – Crediting methods measuring index movements over a greater timeframe than a year or two. The opposite of an annual reset method. Also referred to as a term point-to-point method. Say that the index value was at 100 on the first day of the period. If the calculated index value was at 150 at the end of the period the positive index movement would be 50 percent (150-100/100). The company would credit a percentage of this movement as excess interest. Index movement is calculated and interest credited at the end of the term and interim movements during the period are ignored.

TERM HIGH POINT *(HIGH WATER MARK)* – A type of term end point structure that uses the highest anniversary index level as the end point. Say that the index value was at 100 on the first day of the period, reached a value of 160 at the end of a contract year during the period, and ended the period at 150. A term high point method would use the 160 value – the highest contract anniversary point reached during the period, as the end point and the gross index gain would be 60 percent (160-100/100). The company would then apply a participation rate to the gain.

TERM YIELD SPREAD – A type of term end point structure which calculates the total index gain for a period, computes the annual compound rate of return deducts a yield spread from the annual rate of return and then recalculates the total index gain for the period based on the net annual rate. Say that an index increased from 100 to 200 by the end of a nine year period. This is the equivalent of an 8 percent compound annual interest rate. If the annuity had a 2 percent term yield spread this would be deducted from the annual interest rate (8 percent-2 percent) and the net rate would be credited to the contract (6 percent) for each of the nine years. Total index gain may also be computed by using the highest anniversary index level as the end point.

VARIABLE ANNUITY – A contract issued by an insurance company offering separate accounts invested in a wide variety of stocks and/or bonds. The investment risk is borne by the annuity owner. Variable annuities are considered securities and require appropriate securities registration.

1035 EXCHANGE – The 1035 exchange refers to the section of tax code that allows annuity owners the flexibility to exchange one annuity for another without incurring any immediate tax liabilities. This action is most often utilized when an annuity holder decides they want to upgrade an annuity to a more favorable one, but they do not want to activate unnecessary tax liabilities that would typically be encountered when surrendering an existing annuity contract.

401(K) ROLLOVER – See <u>IRA Rollover</u>

Made in the USA
Columbia, SC
31 August 2021